Information Literacy Education: A process approach

Professionalising the pedagogical role of academic libraries

MARIA-CARME TORRAS

(University of Bergen Library)

AND

TOVE PEMMER SÆTRE

(Bergen University College Library)

Chandos Publishing

Oxford · England

Chandos Publishing (Oxford) Limited
TBAC Business Centre
Avenue 4
Station Lane
Witney
Oxford OX28 4BN
UK
Tel: +44 (0) 1993 848726 Fax: +44 (0) 1865 884448
Email: info@chandospublishing.com
www.chandospublishing.com

First published in Great Britain in 2009

ISBN:
978 1 84334 386 8 (paperback)
978 1 84334 387 5 (hardback)
1 84334 386 X (paperback)
1 84334 387 8 (hardback)

© M-C. Torras and T.P. Sætre, 2009

British Library Cataloguing-in-Publication Data.
A catalogue record for this book is available from the British Library.

Typeset by Domex e-Data Pvt. Ltd.
Printed in the UK and USA.

Printed in the UK by 4edge Limited - www.4edge.co.uk

Til lille Sevard, sønn og sønnesønn

Contents

List of figures and tables

Figures

Tables

About the authors

Dr Maria-Carme Torras is a senior academic librarian at the University of Bergen Library, Norway. She has a PhD in sociolinguistics, and has published within the fields of service encounters and information literacy user education. She has previously lectured in English and linguistics at the Universitat Autònoma de Barcelona.

As well as working as a subject librarian, she designs and teaches information literacy courses. She is also involved in the training of information professionals as user educators. Dr Torras has managed the project 'Learning centres at the University of Bergen Library' (2004–2005), which aimed at developing a process-oriented information literacy education programme for the library. She has also co-managed the project 'Digital Literacy through Flexible Learning' (http://www.ub.uib.no/prosj/DK/index.htm) (2005–2006), partially funded by the Norwegian Open University. The goal of this project was to design an information literacy online tutorial for postgraduate students. The tutorial *Søk & Skriv* (*Search & Write*, http://www.sokogskriv.no/english/index.html) aims at improving students' information literacy by presenting information searching as a process that goes hand in hand with the academic writing process. The tutorial also focuses on the critical, creative, and ethical use of information.

Dr Torras is currently the head of the teaching committee at the University of Bergen Library. Since 2005, she has been a standing committee member of the International Federation of Library Associations and Institutions (IFLA) Section for Information Literacy.

Tove Pemmer Sætre has been a library manager for over 30 years. She was the director of the Hordaland county library for 22 years. For the last 8 years, she has been the library director at Bergen University College, Norway. She has an MA degree in educational theory and libraries and has published within the field of pedagogy applied to both school and academic libraries as learning arenas. She has lectured in librarianship, pedagogy, and didactics in Scandinavia.

Tove Pemmer Sætre has chaired a special Norwegian Library Association board on Library and Information Science (LIS) education and research. She has co-ordinated the National Competence Network for School Librarians, funded by the Norwegian Ministry of Education. She has been chair of the IFLA Section of School Libraries and Resource Centres (2003–2005). Pemmer Sætre is now a standing committee member of the IFLA Section for Social Science Libraries. She was a member of the steering committee for the project 'Digital Literacy through Flexible Learning'. She is a member of the main planning committee for the new Bergen University College campus, where she works on the common learning areas across faculties, which includes a new library.

Acknowledgements

We are indebted to Dr Elisabeth T. Rafste, associate professor at the University of Agder, and Dr Rune Kyrkjebø, senior academic librarian at the University of Bergen Library, for many fruitful discussions and for their useful comments on our manuscript. Thanks are also due to our colleagues with whom we have discussed and reflected on information literacy education at the library. Finally, we would like to thank our families for their support and practical help while we were writing this book.

Introduction

Aim of the book

The aim of this book is to professionalise the educational role of academic libraries. This book puts forward a process-oriented approach to information literacy user education. By user education, we understand both teaching and supervising students. On the one hand, our approach to user education seeks to empower the library practitioner so that she becomes a *professional* and *autonomous* educator (Engelsen, 2006). The professional and autonomous educator makes theoretically founded and independent choices in teaching and supervisory practice. She is willing and capable of examining her own practice critically. On the other hand, our approach encourages the academic library, as a professional community, to build up a common educational platform for information literacy, which will enhance its educational role in the higher education landscape. This book outlines practical ways in which the library's pedagogical involvement in higher education can be strengthened.

Academic libraries face a number of challenges in trying to develop their role as a formal learning arena in higher education. There may be a considerable gap between the academic library's wish to become a teaching institution on a par with the faculty and the academic library's ability to define its educational role at a general policy making or strategy level. Another challenge is that a large number of information professionals are not qualified as educators. User education at many academic libraries is still moving away from the bibliographic instruction paradigm and its focus on library resources. Academic libraries are still heading towards a model of education that focuses on students' needs, and that aims at empowering the student by improving their information literacy, both for legitimate membership in the academic community and for lifelong learning. Information literacy is 'knowing when and why you need information, where to find it, and how to evaluate, use and communicate it in an ethical manner' (Chartered Institute of Library and Information Professionals, 2005). In the information age, although the librarian is still an information expert, a central task of her job should be to facilitate students' learning process so that they become independent information searchers, managers, and producers.

The main target group for library user education represents a challenge too. A new generation of students has entered the universities empowered with a great variety of technical skills, which they have gained both through formal and informal learning. An emergent body of literature (e.g. Lorenzo and Dziuban, 2006; The British Library and JISC, 2008) aims at characterising the information behaviour of the 'Net generation' or 'Google generation'. This generation of today's students have never known life without the internet and feel very much at home in the digital world (Lorenzo and Dziuban, 2006). Nevertheless, concerns arise about the challenges that the Net generation faces in their access to and interaction with information. The British Library and JISC (2008) report that widening access to technology has not improved young people's information literacy. Hughes *et al.* (2007) define it as an information literacy imbalance between 'well-developed digital skills and less developed critical awareness' (p. 59). They have a poor understanding of their information needs, and thus find it difficult to develop effective search strategies and keywords. They do not master critical evaluation of sources. They do not find library-sponsored resources intuitive and prefer the use of searching engines such as Yahoo and Google. They view and power browse documents, instead of reading them. In a similar vein, Walker Rettberg (2007) identifies students' struggles in synthesising information, reflecting critically on their actions and on what they read, and presenting knowledge to others. Lorenzo and Dziuban (2006) share these views. The Net generation experiences serious problems in sorting out valid information from the numerous amounts of sources they are exposed to. In their interaction with information, they fail to blend the necessary skills in finding information, using technology, and thinking critically.

In connection with this, Habermas (2006) raises a further concern. In the internet era, intellectuals have to a certain extent lost their power to create a focus. In the information chaos, knowledge is fragmented. No sage tells the Net generation what is valid information and what is misinformation. We strongly believe that library user education has a crucial part to play here. As The British Library and JISC (2008, p. 33) point out, the challenge is to reverse the process of *dis-intermediation* in the do-it-yourself consumer marketplace. Related to this, the challenge is how to market the role of the library as a safe and authoritative information haven and the need for information literacy education.

Background

All pedagogical practice is the result of specific values, underpinning learning theories and professional experience.

This is also the case in this book. As an instance of pedagogical exercise, this book builds upon the authors' particular values, choice of theoretical background and experience. We will briefly outline them in what follows. We hope that this book will help the information professional make reflected choices on her practice within the educational context she operates in. At the heart of our approach to user education, there are values such as the belief that education should be based on open, reflective, and critical dialogue between students and educators. We believe that students are agents in their development as human beings. We wish to promote academic integrity as a basic principle guiding students' academic practice. As regards our professional experience, the management and practitioner perspective are brought together and underpin the approach we put forth by suggesting a more holistic view on user education. We pay attention to both the library as a professional community in higher education and the information professional as an individual educator.

Our approach to user education is theoretically grounded in the constructivist and the socio-cultural approach to knowledge and learning. Based on the values underlying our view on user education, learning at the library will be maximally enhanced by grounding our practice in these two theoretical perspectives. From the constructivist perspective, knowledge is a continuous process of construction. Students learn by doing and experience (Dewey, 1963), rather than through the information handed to them by the educator. The educator's role in the student's learning process is to create a learning situation and coach students along the way. Learning activities must be based on students' experience, which can lead to the formulation of an engaging problem. Learners gather the necessary information to tackle the problem. They develop and argue for hypotheses and elaborate proposals to solve the problem. They test their hypothesis and solving methods and explore the results obtained. In the reflection that follows, learners look back on the problem and the line of action taken in the light of the insights they have gained throughout the process.

Knowledge is constructed through interaction with the environment. Present learning experiences are assimilated into past mental structures and, by the same token, mental structures gradually change to accommodate the new experience (Piaget, 1971). We also look upon information searching as a process (Kuhlthau, 2004), which intertwines with the academic writing process. The educator's role is to facilitate the student's process of constructing meaning by helping her reflect on how these two processes interact and what kinds of action she can take at each stage in the process.

Situated learning is a concept closely related to the idea of learning by doing and reflection. The educator creates a situational context for learning where learning experiences foster 'real-life' problem solving. For this reason, the approach to information literacy education we propose here should be regarded as incorporated across the curricula. Ideally, incorporation should take the form of *embedment* or *integration* in the sense of Bundy (2004). In this way, students acquire information literacy as they work on their academic tasks. Incorporation of information literacy into the curriculum is an assumption we make when we discuss user education practice in this book. It is, however, beyond the scope of this work to discuss strategies for incorporation of information literacy provision across the curriculum.[1]

The socio-cultural perspective draws upon constructivism, but highlights the construction of knowledge in a context and through interaction with others, rather than through individual processes. Learning is situated in specific physical and social contexts. It is a social phenomenon. Learning takes place by participating in practice communities and having a dialogue with others (Dysthe, 2001). We will elaborate on specific aspects of these theoretical approaches and its consequences for educational practice in Chapters 3 and 4.

Organisation of the book

This book is organised as follows. In Chapter 2, we discuss the position and function of the academic library in the totality of the university community. We attribute its struggle to become a legitimate educational partner in higher education to its complex dual identity in the administrative and academic section of the university. We claim that the educational function of the academic library needs to be formalised through professionalisation both at the organisational and individual level. As a condition on this, the academic library needs to adopt a didactic approach to user education. Among other actions, this calls for a solid pedagogical foundation on which to build up its formal user education. We stress the role of library management in involving the whole library community in this process. We introduce a well-known Norwegian didactic model, Løvlie's (1972, 1974) *pedagogical triangle of practice*, as a reflection model to visualise how education theory can enrich and professionalise library educational practice. The pedagogic triangle of practice challenges and enables the practitioner to reflect on the values, theoretical, and experience-based background that underpins her teaching practice. The reflected work of the professional community at the library is a key factor to strengthen its identity as a formal learning arena.

In Chapter 3, we apply the *didactic relation model*, developed by Norwegian educational researchers Bjørndal and Lieberg (1978), to the context of the academic library. The use of this planning model enables the information professional to explore how pedagogical theory can provide her with concepts and tools that facilitate the design of both specific courses and general educational programmes in information literacy. The model singles out a number of crucial factors – *didactic categories* – in planning education: learning goals, content, learning activities, didactic conditions, and assessment. In this dynamic model, all categories are interrelated. Information professionals can design and carry out courses by contextualising and giving content to each of these categories in relation to the others. The application of these two general didactic models allows the information professional to initiate a didactic reflexion process to assess her own practice. It also provides her with a variety of pedagogical concepts and tools to systematise her thoughts and work, as well as facilitating communication on user education inside and outside the library. Finally, we attempt to strengthen the library practitioner's role as a *professional* and *autonomous* educator by framing the didactic relation model within the pedagogical triangle of practice.

Chapter 4 explores how library supervision can best support the student's research process. We model the supervisory role of the academic librarian based on literature on student supervision, student academic writing, and information searching behaviour. The academic librarian is placed in the supervision constellation that frames the student's research process. In this constellation, we argue that the academic librarian can be a *counsellor* (Kuhlthau, 2004) and process-oriented secondary supervisor who coaches the student in her research process. We claim that supervision at the academic library, both individual and in groups, is a social process and can thus be organised following the principles of *research apprenticeship* (Kvale, 1997). Our model of supervision can be used by both the individual academic librarian and the library professional community to discuss how the academic librarian should intervene in the student's research process and where to draw the boundaries between the librarian's and the academic supervisor's jobs.

In all these chapters, we discuss instances of best and less good practice. Many of these instances are presented through a number of scenarios. They are inspired by our – and our colleagues' – experience with library user education. Through these scenarios, we aim at facilitating the reader's task of relating our model of user education to her professional reality, as well as inspiring and enriching her practice.

Finally, in Chapter 5 we suggest that the academic library, as a formal learning arena, must become a *learning organisation* (Miles, 2003). As such, the academic library is a living organism which has feedback systems and which is able to adapt to the rapidly changing environment of the information age. The library, as an organisation, learns as each of its individual professionals learns in collaborative cultures which share their experiences. Through continuous learning, the library commits itself to change which will improve its performance. We hope that our process-oriented model of information literacy education will help the academic library lay the foundations for continuous learning and improved performance.

Note

1. The reader is referred to Andretta (2005a) and McGuinness (2007), for example, for a discussion of incorporation of information literacy education in the curricula.

2

An educational platform for information literacy

Introduction

In this chapter, we discuss the academic library as one of the learning arenas in the higher education landscape. We characterise the position and function of the library in the university community. We further reflect on why libraries around the world struggle to become a visible and formal part of the higher education learning landscape. Our claim is that the academic library has a dual identity in the university community that challenges its educational role.

In our view, if the academic library is to succeed in becoming an educational partner in higher education on a par with other official partners such as the faculty, it must aim at professionalising the pedagogical role of its practitioners. To achieve professionalisation, the academic library as a professional community needs to lay the pedagogical foundations for its user education. It is necessary for the informational professional to become aware of the complex position and function of the library in the whole of the university community, as well as in relation to each of the faculties it serves. Further, it is necessary for the informational professional to adopt a didactic approach to information literacy education. In this chapter, we introduce a didactic model, Løvlie's (1972, 1974) *pedagogical triangle of practice*, as a tool to reflect on the theoretical foundations, values, and experience on which the informational professional's educational practice builds upon. In this way, the reflected work of the professional community at the library will strengthen the identity of the library as a formal learning arena.

The position of the library in the university organisation

Universities and other higher education institutions consist of an administrative and an academic section. The administrative section deals with political and financial matters on behalf of the whole university society. The academic section includes all the faculties and research centres with their own discipline-specific culture and their own specific views on learning and education. As Figure 2.1 illustrates, the academic library has a dual identity in the university organisation.

Within the administrative section, the library constitutes a visible independent unit with its own professional culture and aspirations. As an *organiser* of information (Kuhlthau, 2004),

Figure 2.1   The academic library in the university community: politics and culture

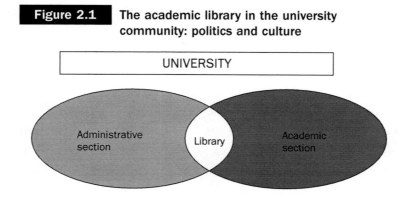

it is clearly well established as an administrative entity. Further, it is of vital importance for library management to have a good close relationship with the administrative section in order to secure sufficient budgets and resources. Within the academic section, the library aims at legitimate participation in the work that each faculty carries out at both curriculum and course level. The library sees the need for close and smooth collaboration with academic staff in order to embed or integrate its user education programme in the curricula. In many countries, this dual picture is even more complex because the library is formally part of the administrative section, but it is physically located and operates within the academic section.

The reasons why academic libraries struggle to be acknowledged and recognised by academic staff are undoubtedly numerous and complex. We regard the dual position of the library in the university organisation as one clear reason why academic staff and library are reluctant to embark on close collaboration projects.[1] This duality undermines the role of the library as an educational partner. For the faculty, the library primarily operates within the administrative section. For this reason, it might look like there is little common ground in terms of competences, responsibilities, and tasks. In the next section, we examine the function of the academic library in the university landscape.

The function of the library as a learning arena

The dual position of the academic library can also explain the fuzzy role that it has traditionally played as a learning arena in higher education. Figure 2.2 reflects the variety of learning arenas constituting the totality of the university landscape,

Figure 2.2 University learning arenas

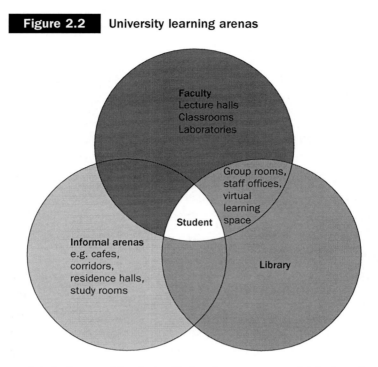

each of them with their distinctive nature, which has been shaped in accordance with its educational aims and needs.

Learning arenas can be described as formal or informal in nature. Students move from one arena to the next in their study day. Their wandering is partially determined by the way their study degree is organised. The lecture hall is typically a formal arena, whereas a campus café is an example of an informal arena. Learning may – or may not – take place in both of them. Students may not be aware of the learning that may take place while talking with their classmates during a lunch break outdoors. Some of the arenas, such as the virtual learning environment, may be common to both the library and faculty. Many universities today use a virtual learning environment as a communication channel between the faculty and students and among students.

Whereas the library is undoubtedly a very visible distinct arena on campus, its function in the learning landscape has been rather unclear. We would like to extend Jackson's (1968) distinction between *hidden* and *formal curriculum* to the context of the library in order to account for the fuzzy function of the library in the campus landscape. As opposed to the formal curriculum, 'the hidden curriculum is not written, does not have explicit objectives, and varies considerably from one school setting to another' (Massialas, 2001, p. 6683). The student learning resulting from the hidden curriculum takes place in parallel with, and in addition to, the learning that results from the *formal curriculum.*

The key question we need to address here is whether the academic library has been mainly a learning arena for the formal or for the hidden curriculum. In our view, there has been a long tradition of hidden curriculum activity in the academic library. Library services have not been integrated in the formal curriculum. Neither the academic staff nor the library staff have been fully aware of how and when the information professional can contribute to the formal curriculum to enhance student learning. As a result, the library has mainly served an archival function, or it has simply been a convenient place to find a quiet desk. Some students might have resorted to the library quite by chance to find relevant information for their work. Some of them might have left the building drowning in references, while others might have been frustrated by the fact that they did not find anything useful. Some other students may have not felt the need for the library at all, as they may have limited themselves to course reading lists or Google searches. In all these cases their learning could have been enhanced if library services (e.g. face-to-face courses, individual supervision) had been integrated into the formal curriculum.

As Jackson (1968) points out, the hidden curriculum also has positive effects on learning. Sætre (2007) discusses the positive effects of the library as an informal learning arena. At the library, students come across new academic texts that stimulate their critical thinking and reflection. They meet other students with whom they can discuss their own work or cooperate in joint assignments. They can benefit from the librarian's expertise in, for example, literature searching and referencing. Information professionals provide students with supervision without the constraints that formal supervision may impose (e.g. time constraints, student's fear of assessment).

The academic library has gradually become more and more interested in defining and promoting its own formal curriculum. We look upon *learning centre* as a concept that emphasises the pedagogical function of libraries (Sætre, 2002), and that may help the information professional reflect on how the formal curriculum of the library should relate to – or be integrated into – the formal curriculum of the disciplines. The concept of *learning centre* encompasses all the informal and formal arenas that make up the microcosmos of the academic library, and all its activities, which may contribute to the hidden or the formal curriculum. Figure 2.3 schematises the multiple learning arenas of the library as a learning centre.

As Fagerli (2000, p. 119) sums it up, libraries, as learning centres, do not just offer access to electronic and printed collections, but also computers and working areas. The modern academic library gives students the opportunity to learn in different spaces and in different ways. They can work individually using a PC in a quiet area. They can use special library rooms to work in groups and to discuss common projects or prepare for class presentations. In addition, libraries offer organised user support services and user education programmes that aim at enhancing optimal

Figure 2.3	The library as a *learning centre*

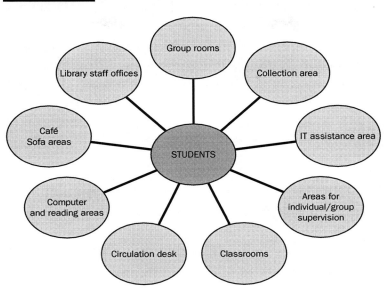

student learning through the interaction of learning resources, user support services, and students. For example, students can attend library courses and obtain individual supervision at the reference desk.

At the same time, the library is also a place to be, a place to socialise (Rafste, 2001). Modern libraries often room enticing café or sofa areas where users can enjoy a break or continue their intellectual work in a more informal setting. Such informal settings can also enhance student learning, when learning is understood as a social phenomenon. As Dysthe (2001, p. 44. Our translation) puts it:

> The role that other people play in the learning process goes beyond stimulating and encouraging the individual construction of meaning. Interaction with others in the learning environment is decisive both as regards what is learnt and how.

Summing up, the academic library is a learning centre consisting of both formal and informal arenas. The library should consider how the available spaces and facilities can best support the hidden and formal curriculum. The focus of this book is on the formal curriculum. In the following sections, we propose ways in which the library can design the formal curriculum and the pedagogical activity that will support it in the formal arenas of the library, such as library classrooms or library staff offices.

A didactic approach to information literacy education

In the following sections, we show how a didactic approach to information literacy education can enable the academic library to design a formal curriculum that is adequately integrated into the formal curriculum of the disciplines. Paving the pedagogical grounds of library user education is a condition for the informed and conscious development of the library as a legitimate formal learning arena. Only when the academic library, as a professional community, has a common understanding of its pedagogical foundations will it be possible to design and carry out user education programmes in information literacy as part of the formal curriculum.

To develop an educational platform for information literacy in practical terms, we will introduce two general didactic models and illustrate how they can be applied in practice. The term *didactics* refers to a theoretical approach to teaching, which is understood as planning, carrying out and evaluating teaching. Didactics includes reflections and decisions concerning the educational goals as well as methods and context. Didactics is a concept within educational theory that builds upon a variety of pedagogical subject fields, such as pedagogical psychology, philosophy, and sociology. The first model, the pedagogical triangle of practice (Løvlie, 1972, 1974), will be presented in this chapter along with examples of how it can be applied to information literacy education. In the next chapter, we will present the second model, the didactic relation model (Bjørndal and Lieberg, 1978). Subsequently, we will come back to the pedagogical triangle of practice, using it as a frame for the didactic relation model.

The pedagogical triangle of practice

The pedagogical triangle of practice (Løvlie, 1972, 1974), represented in Figure 2.4, is a generic tool for professional reflection in planning, carrying out and evaluating teaching

Figure 2.4 The pedagogical triangle of practice (Løvlie, 1972, p. 31 our translation)

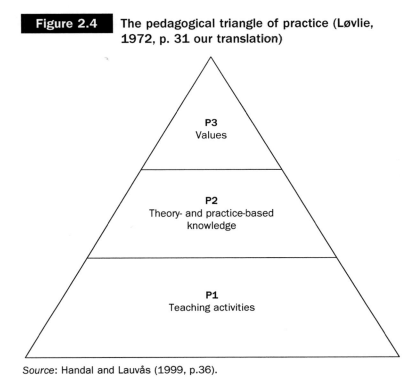

Source: Handal and Lauvås (1999, p.36).

activities both at the theoretical level as well as at the practical level. The model was originally developed as a tool for teacher observation and for giving feedback on performance in teacher training education.[2] Likewise, Løvlie's model can be used by both the individual information professional and the whole professional community at the library to throw light on the complex relationship between theory and practice in library didactics (Sætre, 2002; Rafste and Sætre, 2004).

The model shows that there is more to teacher practice than just what we may observe her doing in the classroom. The three levels in the model display that teaching activities rely on a wide range of ethical, theoretical, and practical reflections and decisions involving the individual professional as well as the whole learning environment. The model challenges teachers to find theory-based and practice-based justifications for what and how they teach. In what follows, we will explore each of the practice levels in the context of library user education. The pedagogical triangle of practice can be used as a tool for professionalising the pedagogical role of the information professional, as well as deciding on how information literacy education should be incorporated into formal learning.

Practice level 3: values

In our library context, the highest level, practice level 3, urges information professionals to decide on what kinds of values and standards they, as individuals, wish to promote in their professional practice. Further, this level invites practitioners to systematically dive deeper into a metatheoretical reflection on the ultimate goals of education, ethical responsibilities, and alternative teaching methods. Sætre (2002, p. 162) exemplifies reflection at this level through questions such as: What is a library? What goals does it have? How does it plan to fulfil its visions and mission? Ethical reflection belongs to practice level 3 too. For instance, at this level, in defining the ultimate aim of information literacy education, both the library and the information professional may choose to endorse the *Alexandria proclamation on information literacy and lifelong learning*:

> Information literacy lies at the core of lifelong learning. It empowers people in all walks of life to seek, evaluate, use, and create information effectively to achieve their personal, social, occupational and educational goals. It is a basic human right in a digital world and promotes social inclusion of all nations (High Level Colloquium on Information Literacy and Lifelong Learning, 2005).

Further, practice level 3 challenges the library as a whole unit to build a common educational platform that mirrors the visions, mission, and goals of the university. As we see it, the following are key factors for successful incorporation of information literacy education in the university curricula:

- The visions and mission of library user education in information literacy must reflect the strategic goals and educational and research priorities of the university in general and the faculties.
- At the same time, library user education must build upon a pedagogic platform supporting the curriculum of the discipline courses in which the library courses are incorporated.

In short, there is a need for alignment at the level of goals and strategies. The goals and strategies that the library establishes for its user education must be in accordance with the goals and strategies described at university management level, faculty level, and discipline course level.

Practice level 2: theory- and practice-based knowledge

Practice level 2 encompasses the whole range of didactic reflections that have to be done by the information professional while planning a complete information literacy programme or just one specific information literacy course. At this level, the information professional as an individual must decide on appropriate theories and values that can be used in the teaching planning process as well as in her practice. The discipline context in which the library teaching takes place will also influence the information professional's choices. They will further be affected by the goals and values at practice level 1. In addition, practice level 2 includes collaboration with the faculty and academic staff in order to define the information professional's roles and tasks as a partner in the students' learning process in practice. Chapter 3 elaborates on this level in detail.

Practice level 1: teaching activities

Practice level 1 refers to teaching and supervising in practice. At this level, information professionals carry out their planned activities. In the 'here and now' of the teaching or supervising situation, the information professional activates her knowledge, puts her skills in use, and manifests her attitudes in interaction with the students. Practice level 1 is 'the moment of truth' in which the library educator faces up to reality. For instance, it is then she realises whether learning goals can be reached and whether the learning activities chosen work out as expected. Unexpected events, such as a technological problem in the classroom, also belong to this level.

After a teaching session, for instance, practice levels 2 and 3 must be revisited in order to reflect on what happened during the session. This is what an academic librarian, Tom, does in the scenario below.

Scenario 2.1

An academic librarian, Tom, is giving a course in literature searching to some MA students who are in the process of writing their research statement. He informs the students that he assumes that, at their level, they all can use the library catalogue and are aware of what they can find there. For this reason, he has not included it in the course and will concentrate on article databases. At that point, the students inform him that many of them are international students who have just arrived in the country. None of them has seen or used the library catalogue before. They would very much like an introduction, as they have been told by their lecturer that the library has a good collection on the students' discipline. Tom is not a great improviser, but he knows that he needs to rework the course plan now, and that some of the planned content and learning activities will have to be dropped. He tries to keep cool, smiles, and mentally reconsiders his course plan to accommodate to the unforeseen student needs. After the teaching, the students thank him for an extremely useful session.

Later, Tom goes through the unexpected incident with some other librarians with whom he participates in a colleague supervision project. They give each other feedback on their teaching experiences. Tom shares with them his reflection about how important it is to be prepared for the unforeseen when teaching. He further points out a weakness in his planning. He should have asked the lecturer about the students' background and state of knowledge in advance. Obtaining this information would have been easy and it would have contributed to planning a much better tailored course for the students. He will bear this in mind in future course planning. Tom's colleagues agree and emphasise the importance of knowing about the students when planning a course.

Tom and his colleagues reflect on an unexpected situation, how Tom coped with it, and what they can learn from it for future course planning. When the information professional succeeds in teaching, it is equally important to reflect on what factors were decisive for the positive learning outcome. Identifying such factors will contribute to successful teaching in future sessions. By revisiting practice level 2 and 3 after teaching, the information professional gradually engages in a constructive process to develop a successful teaching strategy.

Summing up, librarians can use the pedagogical triangle of practice to develop their professional competence and increase their awareness of their role as educators (Sætre, 2002; Rafste and Sætre, 2004). The model provides them with a tool that empowers their legitimacy as reflected information professionals. There is a dynamic relationship between the three levels. The information professional can develop the reflection on her own practice by considering specific instances of courses she has taught, planning of courses, and critical evaluation of planned, carried out and experienced teaching situations. The model throws light on the complex relationship between theory and practice in teaching. It helps the information professional develop her own *practice theory* (Handal and Lauvås, 1999), understood here as the personal ever changing system of knowledge, experience, and values that determine her teaching practice.[3]

Individual practice theory of this kind can, nevertheless, result in difficult communication between practitioners. To prevent this, in Chapter 3 we put forth the use of the didactic relation model (Bjørndal and Lieberg, 1978) as a common model for practitioners to plan teaching and assessment. Developing a common understanding of central pedagogical concepts is a condition for successful professional collaboration between information professionals – and between informational professionals and academic staff – in their user education work.

Laying the foundations for a common information literacy programme

Developing a common information literacy education programme for the library has many advantages. A formalised user education programme ensures better quality in procedures regarding collaboration with the faculty. It makes it clear for all higher education partners what kind of information literacy teaching and supervision the library supports. A formal programme further shows the faculty how the library has interpreted and integrated the general visions and pedagogical goals of the university in its user education.

Within the library, a potential danger when developing a formalised common user education programme is that library staff might feel it is too rigid a frame to work in. They might feel that the programme has been imposed on them by library management, and that it is difficult to interpret, modify, or adapt to their ever changing teaching reality. It is thus of paramount importance that library management involves their teaching library staff in (1) the process of laying the pedagogical foundations of the library user education, and (2) the process of designing a common information literacy programme.

Involving library staff in the education planning process will be beneficial for the institution and their professionals. It will contribute to a common feeling of ownership of the user education programme. Further, it will professionalise the pedagogical role of the librarian.

A good starting point is to ensure that the library staff engages in teamwork that reflects on Løvlie's practice level 3.

In this way, we propose to use Løvlie's pedagogical triangle of practice not just as a tool for the individual information professional, but also for the library as a professional community. On the assumption that library staff are committed and engaged in the process, working together on the pedagogical foundations in order to design library user education will professionalise the information professional in her teaching tasks. This kind of work will challenge information professionals to apply educational theory to their information literacy teaching practice, and will thus give new insights to the library as a special field of teaching practice. Secondly, this work will give the library staff a unique chance to discuss their identity as educators in higher education. It is a fact that not all trained librarians have the necessary (formal) pedagogical/didactic competence to perform teaching activities satisfactorily. This developing work will not only strengthen the library staff's teaching competence, but it will also help management identify areas for further development of the staff and think how the library can meet the needs and live up to the expectations of its different user groups in its education programme.

Finally, flexibility is necessary in information literacy programmes, individual courses, and library supervision in order to meet the changing needs of the users. Practice-based knowledge will provide the information professional with many instances of unexpected changes in syllabi, learning activities, and student conditions. The practitioner can contribute to the developing work with invaluable experience, which will benefit the establishment of goals, contents, and methods. This will contribute to a better suited information literacy programme.

To recapitulate, developing a common information literacy programme for the library will benefit from some preliminary work by means of which the library staff and management lay the pedagogical foundations of their user education. To pave the way, an essential exercise will be reading and interpreting key documents such as higher education laws, government documents giving guidelines for academic libraries, and the university strategic plan. Knowledge about these documents will enable the library to formulate goals and values for its user education that are consistent with those of the other higher education partners. Furthermore, the library's development work must include in-depth discussions about what educational theories are consistent with the overarching goals and values that both the library and the university are committed to. A discussion of educational theory and educational goals and values for the library and their relationship to university views on these matters will be elaborated on in the next chapter.

In the following example, based on Bergen University College documents, the strategy plan of the higher education institution (Excerpt 2.1) is taken as the basis of the library user education guidelines (Excerpts 2.2 and 2.3). The library staff was involved by the library management in the process of writing the library user education guidelines through participation in projects and working seminars.

Excerpt 2.1

Mission

Bergen University College aspires to be an education and research institution that promotes knowledge development, innovation, culture, and lifelong learning. The college aims to have and offer excellent competence, which is sought by students and demanded by society and businesses. The College aims at giving priority to professional degrees, as well as research and development supporting them.

Values

The work at Bergen University College is underpinned by central humanistic values. The College has a learning and work environment where students and staff feel respected and equal, where they are committed to goal-oriented work, and where they are free to participate in open and critical dialogue. Education, research and administration at Bergen University College are driven by sustainable development and high ethical standards.

Source: Bergen University College (2007) (Our translation).

Excerpt 2.2 shows how, in turn, the institution goals and values have been interpreted by the Bergen University College Library and incorporated in the library guidelines for user education. The goals and values of the library have served as a framework for planning its information literacy programme.

Excerpt 2.2

Introduction

In the strategic plan of the College, one general goal is that work will focus on knowledge development, innovation and lifelong learning. The library is an open learning landscape where students and staff can meet a multiplicity of sources which can contribute to reaching such a goal. The condition for this is that sources are searched, read, evaluated and used to create new knowledge. Active and informed searching of scientific information sources and its use can only take place when students and staff have acquired sufficient information literacy to be able to fully use the library's many leads to new and useful knowledge.

> [...] We look upon learning as a constructive process. Learning takes place when one carries out actions and reflects on them. Reflection comprises awareness of one's thoughts and feelings, as well as the actions one carries out. We regard learning as a social process. One learns in their interaction with others [...].
>
> *Source*: Bergen University College Library (2008) (Our translation).

In this example, the library has consciously adopted an approach to education and learning that is consistent with and supports the university college perspectives on lifelong learning and knowledge construction, based on critical and open dialogue. Finally, once the library goals and values for its user education have been stated, the library guidelines for user education go on to specify how the information literacy programme should be organised, including collaboration with the faculty. This is outlined in Excerpt 2.3.

Excerpt 2.3

Each of the College five branch libraries has developed extensive user education and supervision programmes which are tailored to the needs and nature of the study degrees. There is a general framework which is common to all the courses:

The academic staff and the librarian will agree on a course at least 2 weeks before it takes place.

A member of the academic staff will attend the course together with the students.

Courses will be embedded in the degree schedule.

Courses will be planned and carried out based on reflection through the use of the didactic relation model (Bjørndal and Lieberg, 1978).

All libraries will offer at least one progressive user education programme divided up in 3 levels at BA level:

Induction course – Early in the semester.

Search course – Related to specific disciplines, subjects, as well as problem-solving and assignments.

Advanced searching and writing course – At the initial stage of the BA thesis process.

All libraries will offer a user education programme divided up in 2 levels at MA level:

Introduction course – Early in the semester

Specially tailored advanced course – At the initial stage of the MA thesis process

Courses for further education will be tailored for each specific degree.

BA Level 1. *Induction course.* Basic introduction to library organisation and services, based on the library website and portal Mime, as well as introduction to the Bibsys catalogue. Basic introduction to the question of using search engines vs. using licensed scientific databases. Maximum 2 hours in a lecture hall, classroom or computer lab (or a combination of these). Tours of the library will come in addition.

BA Level 2. *Search course.* Related to academic writing (e.g. portfolio assignments) and tailored to discipline or course. Introduction to some databases, including portal Mime. The course will show searching techniques based on relevant examples taken from the students' own work. Individual practice in the searching process with librarian supervision. 1–3 hours in computer lab.

BA Level 3. *Advanced searching and writing course.* Advanced search in some relevant databases. Basic content on academic writing, based on online tutorial *Søk & Skriv* ('Search & Write', www.sokogskriv.no): critical evaluation of sources, referencing and research ethics.

MA Level 1. *Introduction course*. Relevant electronic resources, relevant search examples, referencing, critical evaluation of sources, research ethics, based on online tutorial *Søk & Skriv*.

MA Level 2. *Specially tailored advanced course*. Related to the topics and research questions students will be working on in their MA theses. Teaching based on online tutorial *Søk & Skriv*.

In addition, tailored courses and supervision for smaller groups and for individuals ('Book-a-librarian' service), depending on needs and available resources.

Source: Bergen University College Library (2008) (Our translation).

The work behind the text in Excerpt 2.3 involves moving from Løvlie's practice level 3 to practice level 2. Here it is the library as a community of practitioners, places itself at level 2 of teaching practice. As mentioned earlier, Løvlie's model can thus be used by both the individual practitioner and the professional community as a tool for the professionalisation of their teaching tasks.

Conclusions

This chapter has discussed the position and the function of the academic library in the totality of the university. The duality of the library in terms of its position in the university organisation and its duality as a learning arena (both formal and informal) challenge the legitimisation of its educational role and the design of a formal curriculum. We have argued that the academic library needs to adopt a didactic approach to its user education, which among other actions calls for a solid pedagogical foundation on which to build up its formal information literacy programme. We have used Løvlie's (1972, 1974) *pedagogical triangle of practice* as a didactic model to visualise how education theory can enrich and professionalise library educational practice.

Notes

1. Andretta (2007) discusses other reasons for the challenges the academic library is faced with, among them, failure 'to see information literacy in its wider developmental and social roles' (p. 3), and 'the unwillingness of educators to let go of the traditional transmission of knowledge' (p. 4).
2. Løvlie's model builds upon German pedagogue Erich Weniger's thoughts about the relationship between theory and practice.
3. To a certain extent, *practice theory* corresponds with Stenhouse's (1975) well-known term *strategy*. Stenhouse argues that *strategy* is the basis of a teacher practice. The term *strategy* includes philosophical, psychological, and sociological aspects of teaching, as well as practice-based knowledge. However, unlike the term *practice theory*, it does not take into consideration ethical issues, i.e. Løvlie's practice level 3.

3

Designing process-oriented information literacy education: the library practitioner as a professional and autonomous educator

Introduction

This chapter takes a close look at practice level 2 in Løvlie's (1972, 1974) *pedagogical triangle of practice*, which was described in Chapter 2. Løvlie's practice level 2 comprises practice regarding the planning of courses and the work to be carried out after the teaching (e.g. assessment of student learning). At practice level 2, the informational professional explores how pedagogical theory can provide her with concepts and tools that facilitate the design of both specific courses and general educational programmes in information literacy. Furthermore, at this level the practitioner reflects upon the teaching that has been carried out, for instance, why it was successful or not, how it can be improved in the future. In this context, the educator tends to focus on her role and forgets all the other factors that may play a part in a teaching situation. In this chapter, we apply the *didactic relation model* (Bjørndal and Lieberg, 1978) to the planning of information literacy education at the academic library in order to give the information professional a wider perspective on teaching.

The didactic relation model, developed by Norwegian educational researchers Bjørndal and Lieberg, has proved to be a well suited model for planning education (Engelsen, 2006, p. 47) in the Norwegian context. The model singles out a number of crucial factors and their interaction in planning education. It is, however, in the course of planning a specific course that the teacher will be able to identify and determine which specific factors she needs to bear in mind. We do not aim at an exhaustive description of all categories and identification of all potential factors playing a role in teaching. Each teaching situation is unique, and so is the combination of factors playing a role. The goal of this chapter is to provide a frame for the practitioner to think about course planning in a more holistic way.

In what follows, we examine and illustrate each of the categories comprising the didactic relation model in the context of information literacy education. At the end of the chapter, the didactic relation model is discussed in relation to the other practice levels described by Løvlie (1972, 1974). This final discussion aims at enhancing the professional role of librarians as educators in the academic library.

The didactic relation model

The didactic relation model is intended as a tool for planning and reflection. It assists the information professional in making the analysis of her planning, teaching, and evaluating activities as reflected as possible. The information professional is made to describe and reflect on the key factors that make up a teaching situation and on the ways these factors interrelate. This model empowers the information professional in her practice, as it provides her with a framework to plan education and its evaluation. It increases the information professional's awareness and understanding of her teaching practice.

The didactic relation model builds upon the following didactic categories:

- didactic conditions: student conditions, teacher conditions, administrative conditions
- learning goals
- content
- learning activities
- assessment.

The model is dynamic. All the categories are interrelated and can interact in different ways. According to Bjørndal and Lieberg, this model reflects how teachers think and act when planning their teaching. The advantages of the model are that it clearly illustrates how the choice within one category influences the choices within the others. However, when in use, it should be put into a contextual frame, for instance the curriculum of the subject a specific information literacy

Figure 3.1 The didactic relation model (Bjørndal and Lieberg, 1978, p. 135, our translation)

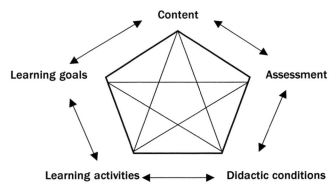

course is supporting. By taking into account the academic context, the didactic relation model is less likely to be used as a non-reflective tool for planning education.

In our institutions, we have experienced that the didactic relation model constitutes a fruitful model for information professionals when planning information literacy courses. It has also proven useful in our collaboration with the faculty to incorporate information literacy education in the curriculum. By adopting this model, the library makes use of a pedagogical jargon that will facilitate communication with the faculty. The use of this model in information literacy education is illustrated in the teaching manuals of Scandinavian online tutorials such as *SWIM*[1] and *Søk & Skriv* ('*Search & Write*').[2]

Summing up, the didactic relation model assists the information professional in her role as an educator. It helps her to plan teaching through a dynamic and creating process. In practical terms, the model facilitates the following teaching aspects:

- the model sorts out the most important factors/categories in teaching;
- it shows that planning is part of the teaching;
- it makes the information professional aware of the fact that the planning cannot totally dictate how the teaching will pan out;
- it makes the information professional aware of the fact that there is no single category that is more powerful than any of the others – any decision regarding one category will affect the others.

We will now illustrate how the model can be applied and reflected upon in terms of information literacy education.

Based upon Bjørndal and Lieberg's categories, library courses can be planned around the following questions: *what, how* and *why* (Engelsen, 2006). *What* refers to goals and content, as well as conditions affecting a specific teaching situation. *How* refers to learning activities, teaching, and assessment methods. *Why* concerns the justification of our choice of goals, content, learning activities, and assessment.

Didactic conditions: what?

There are a number of didactic conditions that make teaching and learning possible or which, on the contrary, may hinder them. Bjørndal and Lieberg highlight the following: student conditions, teacher conditions, and administrative conditions.

Student conditions

Student conditions include their previous knowledge, their skills and motivation. Planning must take into consideration students' previous skills and knowledge about the content of both the information literacy and the discipline course. The information professional should try to find out about what stage the students are at in their study degree and what they are writing about. In addition, it is important to bear in mind psycho-social conditions, for example, students' motivation to attend a specific information literacy course and their emotional state regarding their academic work.

The following scenario exemplifies student conditions, and more specifically, a student's motivation for taking a library course.

Scenario 3.1

In her first term at university, Emily started a BA degree in Italian language. She took a library course in Ethics and Referencing in Academic Writing, which was embedded in a first-year course. In her second term, she has decided to change degree and has now started a BA in English language. A library course is scheduled within one of her introductory BA courses. Emily realises that this is in fact the same library course she attended last semester. However, she admits to the fact that she was rather tired that day and did not really follow it. On the other hand, she experienced some serious referencing problems in her first term assignments, especially when paraphrasing. She thus decides to attend the library course again. She hopes to obtain some useful knowledge and advice there that will help her improve her referencing skills.

Emily realises that she did not benefit from her first course in Ethics and Referencing in Academic Writing. In addition, her unsatisfactory paraphrasing skills have had a negative effect on the quality of her academic work so far. For Emily, the new library course is a 'just in time' (Van Deusen, 1996) course, which will hopefully help her improve her academic writing skills. For this reason, although she has already attended the course once, she is positively motivated to take it again. She hopes to be able to fill in the gaps in her current knowledge about referencing.

It is important to bear in mind that learning conditions may vary over time. The student's psychological state at the point when the course takes place may be a factor conditioning her motivation, as in Emily's case. A library course scheduled late in the afternoon or very early in the morning might demand extra stimulating strategies from the teacher, as students may feel tired and may struggle with their concentration. Thus the teacher might want to take such psychological factors into account when choosing learning activities (see the section 'Learning activities: How?', p. 45).

Students' socio-cultural background may also play a part. For instance, students have busy days. Many of them combine study with work and family. Studies may not be a priority for a number of them. For this reason, they may easily drop courses that are not compulsory. Library courses often fall into the non-compulsory category. On the contrary, courses that have consequences for assessment will be prioritised, e.g. courses where students will be formally assessed or where attendance is controlled.

Teacher conditions

Teacher conditions refer to the information professional's knowledge about both the topic of the library course and the students' specific discipline. For instance, an experienced subject librarian teaching advanced literature searching in specialised databases may feel that she masters the course content satisfactorily. However, she may feel less at ease if the target group is MA students belonging to a discipline in which she has no formal qualifications.

Teacher conditions may also relate to the information professional's attitude towards teaching and her views on pedagogy and user education. For instance, an information professional within the bibliographic instruction tradition will have quite a different approach to teaching information searching than a process-oriented information professional. They both may have similar learning goals for a course in information searching, but the methods and content they choose will vary considerably because of their theoretical views on user education and learning. In Chapter 4, librarians Lena (scenario 4.1) and Paul (scenario 4.2) illustrate these differences. They are giving a similar course for a similar target group, but the learning activities and the content are different. Lena's teaching is anchored in the bibliographic paradigm, whereas Paul has a process-oriented and constructivist focus on learning.

Administrative conditions

Administrative conditions may also have an effect on the teaching/learning situation. To name a few:

- Staff resources
- Duration of the course
- Timing for the course
- Course status: Is the course compulsory? Is it embedded in the curriculum? Is it 'just in case' or 'just in time'?
- Room layout, teaching equipment and materials (PC, projector, hand-outs)
- Administration of the course such as channels to announce the course and registration
- Collaboration with the faculty.

Scenarios 3.2 and 3.3 illustrate the importance of timing as a factor conditioning both teaching and learning.

Scenario 3.2

The library and the faculty have collaborated in designing an introductory course in information searching and library services for freshers. This course is embedded in a compulsory first term course. At the end of the term, academic staff, the contact librarian and student

---

representatives meet up for an evaluation session. In their feedback, student representatives report a timing problem. Some student groups attended the library courses after their discipline course was finished and their course assignment submitted. Student representatives were rather unhappy as not all students had been able to benefit from the same course offer. For a number of students, valuable knowledge for their course assignment was acquired too late. The academic staff and the contact librarian were not aware of this problem. They acknowledged that the timing was unfortunate. Further, they reassured the students that timing for the library course would be carefully reconsidered for the next semester.

Scenario 3.3

A lecturer, Alan, has asked the subject librarian to give a course in advanced literature searching and research ethics for his new MA students. So that students obtain, as soon as possible, all the relevant information and knowledge they will need in their MA studies, he schedules the library course a couple of weeks after the beginning of the semester.

Attendance turns out to be quite low. The course evaluation forms reveal that students attending the course did not find it very useful or relevant. They did not manage to relate its content to their own needs, as they had not decided on their MA topic yet. Their research statement was not due for another few months. Some suggested that the course might have been more useful if it had been offered later on in the semester.

If library courses take place too late or too early in the student's learning process, this may have negative consequences for the student's learning. Scenario 3.3 also exemplifies the relationship between timing and students' motivation (see 'Student conditions', p. 35). The course turns out to be 'just in case', and it is not felt to be relevant by students, as the low attendance and the evaluation forms show. The course would have been more successful, if it had been offered when students actually felt that they needed to look for information or identify ethical problems in their research projects. Timing, just as learning goals and course content, should be a matter of discussion between the librarian and the academic staff. Discussing the students' state of knowledge and their situation in the research process will result in better judgement of course timing.

Scenarios 3.2 and 3.3 further illustrate the importance of evaluation. The students' evaluation of a course through oral or written feedback will contribute to better planning of the next course, at least in terms of timing it, as in this case. Thinking about the teaching situation in terms of the didactic relation model presupposes that the information professional will at all points be flexible and receptive to unexpected or changing factors. Adapting to these 'new' factors will require some improvisation. Encouraging student feedback throughout the course can facilitate adjustment to the unexpected.

Learning goals: what and why?

Learning goals establish *what* the purpose of the course is and describe student learning outcomes. Through them we specify what students should know, what attitudes should be encouraged in them and what they should be able to do after the course. The overarching question that should guide the information professional in establishing the learning goals is *why* the chosen goals are relevant to the student's learning at that point. In more practical terms, the literature traditionally distinguishes three types of learning goals (Bjørndal and Lieberg, 1978; Hiim and Hippe, 1994):

- *Knowledge* goals, which refer to the specific intellectual knowledge that students should acquire.

- *Attitude* goals, which relate to values and attitudes learners should acquire as well as interests that should be encouraged in them.

- *Skill* goals, which refer to psychomotor actions the learner should master.

As Hiim and Hippe (1994, p. 220) point out, the learning goals set for a course will often entail a combination of knowledge, attitude, and skill goals. However, it should be clear for the information professional at the planning stage whether the goal focus will be on intellectual, emotional, or practical aspects. Scenario 3.4 puts forward a formulation of learning goals that combines the three categories described above. The lecturer and the contact librarian specify learning goals for a course in referencing, based both on the problems the lecturer has identified in the students' academic work and on the learning goals of his own course. The library course is meant to have an effect on the students' knowledge, understanding, and attitudes, as well as practically improving their referencing skills.

Scenario 3.4

A lecturer, Charles, has become increasingly concerned about his students' referencing practices. In addition, he has detected a couple of collusion cases lately. He is responsible for a first term course that has the ultimate goal of introducing students to academic thinking, methodology, and writing. Charles is responsible for a large number of students. He feels that he cannot afford the time to take up referencing and ethical questions, as he has a very tight supervision and teaching schedule. For this reason, he is meeting his contact librarian today to explore the possibility of offering his students a basic course in referencing and academic integrity. Charles tells the contact librarian about his students' referencing needs and problems in the context of his course goals. The librarian agrees to give such a course. They discuss what students should know and master after the course. They identify the following learning goals for the library course:

- to understand what 'academic integrity' is and implies
- to understand what practices like plagiarism and collusion are
- to be aware of university rules and regulations regarding plagiarism and collusion
- to understand why referencing is necessary
- to know what needs referencing in their academic work
- to know how to refer to others' work in their own work.

Based on the learning goals, Charles and the librarian move on to discuss course timing and content that can facilitate reaching these goals (see Scenario 3.5).

The information professional should bear in mind the following aspects when working on learning goals. It is of vital importance that there is a correspondence between the goals of the library course and those of the discipline course where it is embedded. Close collaboration between the informational professional and the academic staff is crucial to ensure a good correspondence. In the scenario, the library course goals are consistent with the ultimate goal of Charles' course, which is to introduce freshers to basic academic principles and practices. On the other hand, an open discussion of learning goals between the teacher and the students will benefit the course (Hiim and Hippe, 1993). It will be more motivating for students to follow the course if, from the beginning, they and the informational professional have reached a common understanding of what the aims of the course are and why they are relevant to them at this point in their academic progress.

Content: what?

The question that underlies content planning is 'What am I going to teach this particular group of students?' Although all categories in the didactic relation model interact with each other, learning goals relate to course content very closely. At the course planning stage, it is important to check that the content of the course matches the learning goals. By the same token, all the learning goals should be reflected in the course content. This is what lecturer Charles and the librarian try to do in Scenario 3.5.

Even though the learning goals for a course may be thoroughly established, selecting suitable content is no straightforward matter. When library courses are embedded in the curriculum, it must be decided how general or how discipline specific its contents should be. How to capture the specific nature of the discipline in the library course content can be a challenging task for the information professional, especially if she is responsible for a variety of disciplines and study levels. In any case, the content of the library course should focus on information literacy components that facilitate the student's progress in their academic work at that point. There should be some degree of contextualisation in terms of the content of the discipline course(s) the students are taking and the stage they are at in their

---

Scenario 3.5

The lecturer, Charles, and his contact librarian have established the learning goals for a course in referencing and academic integrity (see Scenario 3.4). Based on these goals, they establish the following content.

Learning goals

- To understand what 'academic integrity' is and implies.
- To understand what practices such as plagiarism and collusion are.
- To be aware of university rules and regulations regarding plagiarism and collusion.
- To understand why referencing is necessary.
- To know what needs referencing in their academic work.
- To know how to refer to others' work in their own work.

Course content

- Introduction to concepts 'academic integrity' and 'academic misconduct'.
- Introduction to university rules and regulations regarding plagiarism and collusion.
- Referencing in the text.
- Listing references.
- Use of Harvard style sheet to document sources.

---

academic work. It is important that after the information literacy course, the evaluation process assesses whether there was a satisfactory match between goals and content.

Time, as discussed above, is a didactic condition that may constrain teaching. For instance, the faculty may feel that the academic curriculum calls for a busy lecture and seminar schedule. It may not be possible to allot the library all the time it would ideally want to devote to its embedded user education. For this reason, it is important for the information professional to single out *core* content for the library course. As Karjalainen *et al.* (2006) argue, defining core course contents is fundamental in curriculum development. If time is scarce, the informational professional might be tempted to cover all the planned content by increasing the pace of teaching. This is likely to be an unfortunate decision. In scenario 4.1 (see Chapter 4), Lena's exhaustive and non-contextualised instruction in the library databases may result in undesirable learning outcomes. It is most likely to lead to surface learning. In the worst case scenario, students may feel overwhelmed by the course content and conclude that library resources are inextricable. This might lead them to discard the library resources and to firmly believe that Google and Wikipedia are more convenient resources.

Learning activities: how?

Learning activities refer to the actions the students and the teacher carry out in a learning situation. In curriculum jargon, they are often referred to as methods and techniques (e.g. to work in groups, to collect, to summarise) or processes (e.g. to investigate, to assess, to define). Didactic conditions such as number of students and availability of classrooms play a part in the selection of learning activities. For instance, small group activities are not likely to be successful in a course for hundred students that takes place in a big lecture hall. Individual activities might be a better alternative in this case. At the same time, the learning activities used by academic staff will be largely dependent on the faculty and discipline views on learning and teaching and thus what the curriculum describes. To a certain extent, the choice of learning activities will also be affected by the teacher's own views on teaching and learning.

Reflection is a central activity in learning understood as a constructive process. From a constructivist perspective, the acquisition of information can be looked upon as an integrated activity in the research process, and ultimately, in the student's learning process:

> [...] learners question knowledge acquired earlier, opposing it with information that may shed light upon a topic and contribute to a new understanding of the topic, information is seen as a means of bridging a gap between existing knowledge and a problem to be solved. (Blaabjerg, 2005, p. 1).

Interestingly, Blaabjerg identifies an overlap of methods, when information searching is seen as integrated in the learning process. For instance, the activities involved in identifying information gaps may actually be quite similar to those of defining the core of the problem at hand. As Blaabjerg (2005, p. 2) points out, library teaching and supervision should '(...) facilitate learner's reflection on their prior experiences of learning and information searching process'. Scenario 3.6 gives an example of how student reflection can be promoted through information literacy learning activities.

Scenario 3.6

A group of students taking a BA course in applied linguistics are working in pairs to produce a leaflet on how bilingual children's language acquisition can be promoted. This informative leaflet is meant to be distributed to bilingual or multilingual families through schools and nurseries in an officially monolingual society. As a formal requirement to this

---

course, students are expected to attend an information searching course at the library and to complete the following assignment on their information searching process.

Assignment: a leaflet on how bilingual children's language acquisition can be promoted

1. Define your topic. What specific question(s) are you going to address in the leaflet?
2. Use a writing technique such as mindmapping or brainstorming to organise your first thoughts on your topic.
3. Plan your search.

   3.1. Write a list of keywords with synonyms. If you think you will be using databases in languages other than English, include keywords and synonyms in that language too.

   3.2. Write keyword combinations. Choose one of your combinations and justify your choice of keywords in it.
4. Explore the available databases in the library and consider what you find.

   4.1. Select two databases that are relevant to your work and justify why they are relevant. Specify the keyword combinations used.

   4.2. Select three references that are relevant to your work and justify their relevance.

   4.3. If you did not obtain any hits, or any good hits, in any of the databases, how did you improve your search? What was the result?

The assignment has been designed by the library subject specialist and the lecturer jointly. The subject specialist is responsible for marking the assignments. She gives students specific feedback on their work and gives them a pass or a fail. Students who fail are given the opportunity to rewrite the assignment. The assignment contributes to the student's final assessment. The university virtual learning environment is used for handing in the assignment, marking it, and for communication between the subject specialist and the students after the course.

In their answer to question 4.3, one student pair reported considerable frustration when searching in the library catalogue. Their keyword combinations did not yield any relevant hits. They concluded that Google was a much more relevant information resource in this case, as searching with any keyword combination yielded a vast number of hits. Some of the hits included official documents dealing with bilingual children. The students looked upon these documents as relevant sources of information for their work. They expressed disappointment in the library catalogue, as they had not been able to find out about them through it.

As part of her feedback, the information specialist pinpoints a number of problems in the students' formulation of keywords, such as the choice of too general or too specific keywords and the combination of too many keywords. She suggests some lines of action and asks the students to resubmit questions 3 and 4 again. Regarding question 4.3, she specifically asks the students to compare the results yielded by Google and the library databases.

This kind of assignment illustrates how students' metacognition and reflection on their own information searching practices and the process they have gone through can be encouraged. Metacognition can be defined as knowledge on how, why and when it can be appropriate to use specific cognitive strategies, as well as control of one's strategy use through monitoring of one's work and ability to shift strategy if necessary, to evaluate results and one's performance (Throndsen, 2002). Metacognitive strategies are deployed to plan, monitor, control, and evaluate the use of cognitive strategies.[3] Cognitive strategies are goal-oriented activities (thoughts and actions) that the learner deploys to enhance her learning or improve her task solving (Bråten, 2002). They are deployed when the learner experiences a mismatch between a learning goal and her current knowledge or competence. Pressley *et al.* (1987) argue that a continuous monitoring of how chosen strategies are working in the learning process gives the learner the necessary information to assess whether she should continue to use a specific strategy, or whether it should be modified or replaced. Bråten (2002) presents research evidence showing that advanced use of cognitive strategies is essential for successfully accomplishing tasks based on learning from written sources. It is thus important for the information professional to think about learning activities that help students develop their metacognition.

In the scenario above, metacognitive activity is encouraged by asking the students to describe how the task was solved and justify their actions throughout the process. In the discovery learning method, the process is just as important as the product. As Bjørndal and Lieberg (1978) point out, processes represent ways of thinking and acting that can be essential to further learning. They can also relate to positive values and attitudes that are important for the learner's development. In Scenario 3.6, the students are asked to go back in their searching process after some *scaffolding* (Wood *et al.*, 1976). In order to support the students, the librarian spots the problem and suggests a possible line of action, which the students need to explore and try out.

Further, the scenario above practically shows how the subject specialist can obtain student descriptions and reflections on their searching process in connection with their specific academic work. The information professional gains insight into the students' searching process. She is thus provided with material to further contextualise the searching process in her teaching and supervision. It can also give her a good discussion example to introduce other information literacy related issues such as critical evaluation of sources. For instance, this example can be used to discuss how Google hit lists compare with library catalogue hits in terms of reliability, authority, relevance, and so on.

The assignment in the scenario above exemplifies most of the learning activities Bjørndal and Lieberg (1978) include in their typology. It involves:

- *Manual/instrumental* activities, such as searching for literature in the library.

- *Process* activities, e.g. evaluating a source critically, formulating good keywords, refining searching techniques.

- *Social* activities, such as establishing a dialogue between the students (pair work) and between the students and the information professional.

Bjørndal and Lieberg also distinguish *experience* activities, i.e. activities that focus on emotional aspects of the learning process. For example, one such activity, based on group discussion, could aim at helping students cope with the uncertainty and anxiety they may feel at the beginning of an MA thesis project (see Chapter 4, section on 'Student needs and challenges').

Bjørndal and Lieberg discuss a number of crucial aspects to bear in mind when designing learning activities. They emphasise that learning activities must correspond with the content, learning goals, didactic conditions, and assessment of a given teaching situation. They further point out that learning activities should ideally cover all the learning goals of a course. Not all learning goals can be reached by just delivering content. Carroll (2002) is a strong supporter of this view in her handbook for deterring plagiarism in Higher Education. It is not enough to tell students about plagiarism.

It is necessary to work on this topic through appropriate student activity.

Consider the following learning activity, which the librarian has chosen for the course described in Scenario 3.5 above. This activity, which is mainly a process activity, is meant to help students reach some of the knowledge goals described in Scenario 3.5, namely to know what needs referencing.

Learning activity[4]

'Where do we need to use a reference?' In the text below, the references to others' work and ideas that the original author used have been removed. Decide and justify where we need to use a reference.

> Two assumptions help situate my perspective on culture and communication. First, communication is the medium by which we come to know things in personal and professional life. Knowledge is socially constructed through language and other symbolic systems, and language – in functional approaches to contexts of situation – is a socio-cultural resource constituted by 'a range of possibilities, an open-ended set of options in behaviour that are available to the individuals in his existence as social man'. My second assumption about language use is that its essence is always in dialogue, irrespective of the format it may take (written, spoken, formally monologic or dialogic). This may be interpreted in two mutually non-exclusive ways. First, it means that the meanings embedded in linguistic resources emerge from their uses in different contexts and are shaped by the cultural, historical, and institutional forces that characterise those contexts.

(*Source*: Bondi 2007, p. 54)

Another important aspect to consider is student relevance. Learning activities that students can relate to their own experience or need will be felt as more meaningful and useful. For instance, let us imagine that a group of students are asked to evaluate a text critically based on criteria such as reliability and authority. To make the activity more relevant to the student, the information professional can allow the students to choose their own text, instead of providing the same text for all of them. This will result in a more flexible activity, where students can have their say and contribute their individual interests, preferences, and alternative ways of solving the same task.

In planning user education, the information professional will naturally choose activities or methods that can best promote students' information literacy in a given learning situation. However, it is recommended that the information professional considers how her choice of learning activities compares with those chosen by the faculty. These activities may blend in well with those chosen by the academic staff, or they may somehow represent conflicting views on learning. For instance, a library course based on problem-based learning might make collaboration with the academic staff challenging, if academic staff works within a transmission model of teaching based on lectures and a final exam. In addition, lack of harmony between the faculty and library learning activities may lead to unreasonable working demands on the students. By contrast, if the discipline course builds upon project work and the embedded library course relates group work activities to the students' project, learning activities will enhance the students' learning progress.

Assessment: how and what?

Assessment must be taken into consideration in the planning of a course. It must be tuned in with all the other didactic categories. Assessment can be defined in a variety of ways.

In order to operationalise this category, Engelsen (2006) suggests focusing on the following four key questions:

- What is the goal of the assessment?

- What will be subject to assessment?

- What criteria will be used for assessment?

- When will the assessment take place?

One type of assessment we would like to discuss here is the way in which the information professional may determine whether – and to which extent – students have reached the established learning goals. This is *goal-related* assessment,[5] which measures student performance in relation to the learning goals established (Bjørndal and Lieberg, 1978). In Bjørndal and Lieberg's view, assessment is a means to an end. Its ultimate goal should be to enhance learning. For this reason, assessment should be well integrated in the learning process. Ideally it should be a collaborative effort between students and library and academic staff. If the aim is goal-related assessment, at the planning stage it may be useful to elaborate on the four questions above by deciding on the following:

- What aspects of the student performance will be focussed on? What skills, attitudes, and/or knowledge will be assessed? Will the students' process or/and the student's final product be assessed?

- What method will be used? (e.g. final exam, project, portfolio).

- Will students be assessed individually or as a group?

- Will student performance in relation to library learning goals be assessed independently or as part of the assessment carried out in the discipline course or degree the library course is embedded in?

- Who will carry out the assessment? The information professional, the academic staff or both?

- When will the student be assessed? At the beginning of the course (e.g. diagnostic test), through final or continuous assessment?

Scenario 3.6 above illustrates a specific case of assessment, which is the result of the informational professional and the lecturer's decisions at the planning stage. Assessment focuses on the students' information searching process, which comprises both their searching skills and their capacity to reflect on their course of action. The assessment is goal-related. The information professional is responsible for marking the assignments, but this assignment is part of the continuous assessment of the discipline course, which is based on portfolio work. Students are assessed in pairs in the belief that learning is a social activity (see Chapter 4) and that dialogue increases students' metacognition.

Planning assessment may be perceived as a challenging task for the library. The library course may not be compulsory and no assessment of learning outcomes related to the library course goals may be specified in the academic course the students are taking. In many cases, the information professional only sees students in one or two sessions. Further, some information professionals may feel a lack of competence or resources to plan and carry out systematic assessment. Lack of time or collaboration with the faculty might also lead the information professional to neglect planning on the assessment front. In our opinion, the didactic relation model can help increase the information professional's awareness of the importance of planning assessment. For instance, relating assessment to learning goals at the planning stage can be a rewarding exercise. Student motivation and library course attendance rates may increase if: (a) explicit information literacy learning goals are included in the goals of a discipline course, and (b) information literacy goals are included in the goal-related assessment of the discipline.

Framing the didactic relation model within the pedagogical triangle of practice

In Chapter 2, we introduced Løvlie's pedagogical triangle of practice as a professional reflection model to build up an educational platform for information literacy. In this chapter, we have introduced Bjørndal and Lieberg's didactic relation model, which is essentially a model for planning teaching. In planning and carrying out information literacy education, these two didactic models should not be used independently of each other. The dynamic combination of these two models

Figure 3.2   The didactic relation model framed within the pedagogical triangle of practice (P = practice level)

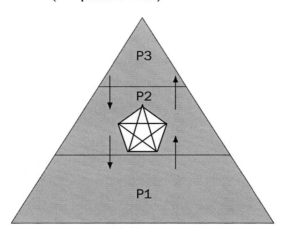

will enable the library practitioner to become a more reflected and professional educator, which will in turn enhance the educational role of the academic library.

The information professional will be able to dive deeper into Løvlie's practice level 2, if she places the didactic relation model within the broader context of the pedagogical triangle of practice, as Figure 3.2 sketches out. When planning teaching, it is necessary to bear in mind the core values and mission of the institution (practice level 3), as well as the theoretical perspectives underpinning the information professional's teaching. Throughout all the phases of her teaching practice, the information professional can navigate freely between the three practice levels. After the teaching, at practice level 1, the information professional can revisit all the didactic categories at practice level 2 to look back on her teaching experience in relation to the theory- and practice-based knowledge she owns at this level. She can further revisit practice level 3 to assess whether what happened in the classroom conforms to the core values and mission of the library.

The information professional should carry out *summative* assessment (Bjørndal and Lieberg, 1978), that is, evaluation that takes place after the teaching and comprises students' performance and opinions, the course, the teacher's performance, and teaching materials. The goal of summative assessment should be to obtain a description of what the teaching situation was like, and why it turned out to be that way, so that the information professional can enrich her pedagogical competence and improve her future teaching (Engelsen, 2006). Systematic assessment like *summative* assessment, which takes into consideration all the didactic categories, enriches the practice-based knowledge at practice level 2. Practice level 1 feeds practice level 2 after a teaching situation and, in this way, future planning and teaching will be improved.

For assessment to be meaningful, we need to carefully decide on its goals, focus, and criteria. For instance, the assignment in Scenario 3.6 will allow the librarian and the lecturer to measure learning outcomes related to the established goals. At another level, the following evaluation form will give us information about the students' experience of their own learning, if we aim at including this metareflection in the general assessment process (see Hiim and Hippe, 1993).

Course evaluation form

- What have you learnt in this course?
- What do you know/can do/are aware of now that you didn't know/could not do or were not aware of before taking this course?

The following texts are real samples of students' answers to the questions above. The questions were used in an evaluation form that students were asked to complete after a first-year basic course in referencing and ethics.

Student evaluation samples

- 'I think that the course was very good because I did not know anything about how to cite or write a list of references'.
- 'I learned about plagiarism, which turned out to be a lot more than I thought it was, and I know now how to avoid it. I also know how to refer to sources in the text.'

> - 'After this course I have become more aware of mistakes in citing works that I did not know about before. I have also become more aware of coming across as an independent reader while writing my term paper'.
> - 'A new understanding of how important it is to follow the rules. I didn't know that plagiarism could be so much [*sic.*]. It is easy to forget to reference your sources, so from now on I will keep this in mind'.

The evaluation text samples illustrate a reflection exercise on the part of the student. Further, they give the information professional an insight into the student's own perceptions of learning after that specific course. This insight may be useful in considering to what extent course goals have been achieved. For instance, one of the goals of this course was to increase students' awareness of the importance of referencing and their understanding of what academic integrity and plagiarism are. Alternatively, the information professional may be interested in assessing her own performance and other – negative and positive – aspects of her course management. Exploration of such aspects may be easier to undertake if the evaluation form includes the ratings or questions exemplified in Appendix 1 (see pp. 99–100).

Conclusions

In this chapter, we have explored in detail the planning that takes place at Løvlie's practice level 2, also bearing in mind levels 1 and 3. We have discussed and exemplified Bjørndal and Lieberg's didactic relation model as a useful model to plan library courses in information literacy. The didactic relation model encourages the information professional's reflection on her teaching practice. Its use enriches her theoretical reflection on planning courses, her choices, and their justification. The model further enables the information professional to assess her teaching practices in the light of new experience and better theoretical insight.

The didactic relation model puts forth a number of categories that can help informational professionals systematise their thoughts and their work. The categories reflect factors that the information professional should bear in mind in her planning because they may condition the teaching. By the same token, the choices made by the informational professional when dealing with the different categories should reflect both her pedagogical background and her institution's. Just as importantly, these categories constitute a common ground in the teamwork going on in the library as well as in the library contact with the faculty. These categories constitute a common terminology that facilitates communication inside and outside the library, and that is crucial for satisfactory collaboration.

The use of Bjørndal and Lieberg's model within the context of the pedagogical triangle of practice contributes to making library practitioners *professional* and *autonomous* educators (Engelsen, 2006). It helps information professionals make theoretically founded and independent choices and decisions in their teaching practice. If we apply the views in Stenhouse's (1975) seminal work on the professional teacher, professionalising the pedagogical role of library practitioners entails turning them into *researching teachers*. The practitioner must become a 'researcher' in her own class, which means that she should be:

- systematically critical of her own teaching
- willing and capable of examining her own teaching
- willing to apply theory to her teaching practice

- willing to allow other teaching practitioners to observe and discuss her teaching.

Engelsen (2006) argues that a critical attitude to the relationship between teacher and curriculum can help bridge the gap between what the curriculum describes in theory and the teaching reality that the teacher experiences. The information professional must test and adapt the curriculum to the reality of her classroom.

Notes

1. See the *SWIM Pedagogical Manual*, available from http://www.swiminfo.dk/pdf/paedagogik.pdf/.
2. See the *Søk & Skriv Pedagogical Manual*, available from: https://bora.uib.no/bitstream/1956/2205/1/SOS_kursholdere.pdf/. See also Skagen *et al.* (2008).
3. Metacognitive strategies are an essential component in *self-regulated learning*, as defined from a social-cognitive perspective (see for instance Bråten, 2002).
4. This activity has been inspired by the materials handed out by Jude Carroll at the workshop 'Students and plagiarism – a story in three parts', held at the University of Bergen, Norway, 12–13 March 2007.
5. Engelsen (2006, p. 121) distinguishes between goal-related, individual-related, and group-related assessment, depending on the criteria chosen to measure student performance.

4

Facilitating the student's research process: the academic librarian as a supervisor

Introduction

Library user education comprises both teaching and supervising. This chapter reflects on and defines the information professional's extended educational role as a supervisor at the academic library. The central question that this chapter addresses is how library supervision can best support the postgraduate student's research process. The information professional's pedagogical role is characterised on the basis of postgraduate students' needs and struggles. The reason why we focus on the postgraduate student in this chapter is that, at this level, the student is engaged in a more comprehensive, demanding, and long-term research process. As a consequence, the relationship between the student and the supervisor becomes closer and more long term. Based on research on postgraduate student supervision, we put forth a model of library supervision to extend the educational role of the academic librarian. In our view, supervision of postgraduate students does not only require information expertise from the librarian, but also academic qualifications in a discipline. For this reason, we use the more specific term 'academic librarian' rather than the more general term 'information professional' in this chapter. Nevertheless, this supervision model may also be applied to the supervisory tasks of other information professionals at the library and at undergraduate level.

This chapter is organised as follows. First, the information needs and challenges of the postgraduate student are identified in the context of her research process. Secondly, a number of research supervision models are discussed with the aim of exploring how the librarian can best support the postgraduate student's research process. Finally, four scenarios are discussed that illustrate alternative supervisory roles in practice. The scenarios aim at encouraging the information professional to reflect on their supervisory role in the student's information search process, and how supervision in this process can also support the student's writing and research process. The conclusion brings up some challenges that librarians and their institutions may experience in extending their role as supervisors and teaching partners in higher education.

The postgraduate student's research process

Individual and group supervision at the academic library should be guided by students' information needs and challenges. Being aware of the student's research process and the challenges she is confronted with is a condition for designing effective supervision. The following sections draw upon research on both academic writing and information searching behaviour in order to define the difficulties that students experience in the research process.

Information searching and writing as intertwining processes

Handal and Lauvås (2006) describe the research process of a postgraduate student in the humanities and social sciences as consisting of the phases schematically described in Table 4.1.

The research process can be looked upon as an overarching process incorporating information searching and writing activities, as well as other research activities (e.g. collecting data). Students go through an information searching process that intertwines with their writing process. The writing process is understood here as the working phases from choosing – or being given a topic – to producing a final academic text for assessment (Dysthe *et al.*, 2000, p. 39). Dysthe *et al.* (2000, p. 46) sum up the connection between information searching and writing as follows. Academic texts build upon other texts. For this reason, writing is heavily dependent on reading literature about the selected topic. Selecting literature is dependent on good literature searching. Nevertheless, this does not mean that writing should exclusively start after conducting information searching and reading the gathered literature. Dysthe *et al.* points out that defining information or literature needs will become an easier task after some writing has taken place. Writing before reading will help the student find her own voice and formulate her own thoughts better, without feeling overwhelmed by

Table 4.1   **Phases in the postgraduate research process in the humanities and social sciences**

Choice of topic	Defining research question	Reading Data collection	Draft writing	Draft rewriting and editing	Closure

Source: Handal and Lauvås (2006, p. 67. Our translation).

what the authorities in the field have said. Further, writing while she is reading will help her establish a dialogue with the literature, gain her own understanding of it and formulate her own thoughts about it.

The information searching process

The phases that Handal and Lauvås (2006) identify in Table 4.1 roughly match those described in Table 4.2. In Table 4.2, we can see how the information searching process, as described by Kuhlthau (2004), relates to the writing actions and other activities in the totality of the research process.

Kuhlthau (2004, p. 44) characterises information searching as a process that '(...) incorporates three realms: the affective (feelings), the cognitive (thoughts), and the physical (actions) common to each stage'. It is important to point out that Kuhlthau's model does not describe a process that is exclusively linear. Foster, who analyses the behavioural patterns of the information seeker, concludes that '[...] activities remain available throughout the course of the information seeking' (Foster, 2004, p. 228).

In the first stage (see Table 4.2), students recognise an information need, try to understand the task or assignment, and consider possible topics and approaches. At stage 2, they select a general topic and consider what approach to take. Topic selection will be dependent on a number of factors such as personal interest, time and information available as well as supervisor's interests. Students typically feel uncertainty during these two stages (see 'Student needs and challenges', p. 69), but they feel some optimism once they have decided on a topic. These first stages are characterised by creative idea development (Aalborg University Library, 2006). A number of ideas are generated and developed. The ideas contemplated by the student in

| Table 4.2 | Information searching and writing as intertwining process in the student's research process |

Information search process (Kuhlthau, 2004)		Writing actions	Other actions or strategies
Stage 1	Task initiation	Brainstorming Mind mapping Writing 'for thinking'	Reflecting on research ethics
Stage 2	Topic selection		
Stage 3	Pre-focus exploration	Annotated bibliography First outlines Project statement	
Stage 4	Focus formulation	Listing and structuring keywords	
Stage 5	Information collection	Draft writing Writing 'for presentation'	Critical evaluation of sources Referencing
Stage 6	Search closure	Conclusion writing Final writing up	Ethical use of sources Presenting one's work

Source: Adapted from Torras and Skagen (2006).

this phase will help her define her information needs and start her searching process.

Pre-focus exploration is according to Kuhlthau the most difficult stage in the process. Students try to investigate their general topic so as to obtain an overview of it, rather than going into depth. They try to extend their personal understanding and define key concepts in order to narrow down the topic. They start formulating a preliminary research question. Uncertainty and confusion might be quite dominant feelings while students try to find a focus for their general topic. Relating new information from different sources to previous knowledge is not a smooth process, and even less so when one does not really know what exactly one is going to write about. Students locate relevant literature and read to learn about the general topic, but they might easily feel after a while that they are drowning in a sea of references without a specific purpose. Pre-focus exploration is also a creative phase (Aalborg University Library, 2006). Ideas and thoughts are explored on the surface, connected to each other and grouped into general themes. Different ways of presenting the problem area are seized up. Decisions are made on what aspects should be included or left out in the research question.

Feelings of clarity, certainty, and confidence increase from the fourth stage, i.e. focus formulation. Gradually students succeed in establishing a concise problem area, and thus in finding their own 'plot of land' within the general topic. They form a focus and can define their research question, albeit still in a preliminary way. It is thus easier for the student to define what information gaps need to be filled in.

At the subsequent stage, information collection, students gather information relevant to their specific research question. This stage calls for critical and analytical research (Aalborg University Library, 2006). The research question is investigated on the basis of pertinent scientific information. Students dive deeper into the problem by conducting in-depth information searching. The data students work with are analysed and researched critically. The research is documented in drafts that gradually become final chapters. Students feel more clarity. They can articulate their information needs much more accurately at this stage. They work out keywords and keyword combinations out of their research question. They are ready for comprehensive searches in relevant scientific information resources. The scholarly literature they find expands various theoretical and methodical aspects of their research question.

At the final stage, students close the search. They may feel that they have enough information or that the deadline is simply too close. They thus need to do the final writing up and prepare for submission. The conclusion in their research work is placed in a broader perspective and new research areas or problem definitions are sketched out. In the conclusion, students show their overall knowledge of the field and their ability to place documented research in relevant new contexts. Students have gathered a body of literature during the whole process. They might now use some of the references they had initially put aside in order to find alternative perspectives on their treatment of the topic and suggest new lines of research. Whether satisfied or not, the student feels relieved.

The writing process

Dysthe *et al.* (2000) highlight the importance of writing throughout the research process. Writing helps the student formulate, register, develop, and structure her thoughts. When the student goes back to her text, she resumes her train of thought and discovers new associations. In addition, writing helps internalise knowledge, as well as activating the unconscious. Dysthe *et al.* distinguish two types of writing, each of them serving a different purpose: 'writing for thinking' and 'writing for presentation'. Writing for thinking is private, informal, and exploratory. It is creative as it helps the student come up with ideas. It stimulates and clarifies her thoughts about a topic. It is process-oriented. Writing for thinking is a good strategy for preventing writer's block. Students often try to produce writing for presentation from day 1, texts that should be good enough for submission as a final product, which may lead to writer's block. In the research process, 'writing for thinking' will gradually give way to 'writing for presentation', although students are likely to alternate between creativity and criticism throughout the writing process. Writing for presentation is formal. Its aim is to communicate knowledge to a reader (e.g. the examiner, the academic community). It is product-oriented and it reflects critical-analytical thinking.

Conclusions

To recap, it is through the intertwining information searching and writing activities that students advance in their research process and in the construction of meaning. Students start by writing texts mainly for themselves (e.g. mind mapping, brainstorming), which help them define their focused topic and research question. These initial texts are useful tools to find and define central concepts related to their topic. Through the elaboration of these concepts, students will be able to identify keywords that can subsequently be used as search words in their information searching activity. This is work where the academic librarian can offer good assistance.

By the same token, the outcomes of information searching will influence the development of the student's topic interest and research question. The initial texts written for oneself are the basis for more elaborated texts written for others, such as chapter drafts that are submitted to the supervisor and paper presentations for seminars. Through these more elaborate texts, the student can articulate their specific information needs more accurately, refine their searches and explore more specialised databases that will provide them with pertinent information. The intervention of the academic librarian at this point should aim at facilitating this in-depth searching process.

Student needs and challenges

The literature on academic writing (e.g. Dysthe *et al.*, 2000; Kamler and Thomson, 2006) and our own library teaching and supervision experience reveal that the postgraduate student faces a number of challenges in her research process, such as:

- Narrowing down a research question from a general topic
- Dealing with large amounts of available sources
- Evaluating information analytically and critically
- Using terminology correctly
- Using information creatively, that is, transforming it into own knowledge, which is communicated in the student's work
- Structuring the text in a logical way
- Constructing and supporting arguments
- Expressing own views and supporting them
- Drawing conclusions
- Using information ethically
- Referencing.

The aspects mentioned above involve essential skills that often are assumed to be tacit knowledge in academia. They are not necessarily taught in an explicit way. However, if students do not master these skills, their research work quality may drop considerably. The academic librarian has expertise and competence to support the student in mastering some of these skills, such as finding relevant information, evaluating it critically and referencing it correctly. Students' texts, like all other academic texts, build upon other texts. Dysthe *et al.* (2000, p. 25) point out that building up one's work on others' texts requires the following skills from the student:

- Selecting what information to read
- Reading with different aims
- Taking useful notes
- Summarising or paraphrasing others' thoughts and views acceptably
- Using the information read in context of one's research question
- Using sources to support one's arguments
- Documenting the sources that are cited or referred to.

Library supervision should support the student in developing all the skills that enable them to use information sources in her own writing. A mutual understanding between the academic supervisor and the academic librarian of what this support should be like will result in better overall assistance for the student. The academic supervisor and the academic librarian may decide that the librarian will be entirely responsible for promoting certain skills such as selecting information, paraphrasing, referencing, while the academic supervisor will be entirely responsible for other skills such as developing and supporting arguments. They may further decide that they can both work jointly on promoting some other skills. For instance, in terms of using terminology correctly, the librarian can help the student identify key concepts in her research question and find background literature to define and relate them. The academic supervisor can discuss with the student whether her choice of terminology is adequate and consistent with the theoretical background the student has chosen.

As described above, there is also a psychological dimension to the research process. Kuhlthau (2004, p. 92), among other researchers (e.g. Dysthe, 2006), reports that students feel uncertainty at different stages of their research process:

> Uncertainty is a cognitive state that commonly causes affective symptoms of anxiety and lack of confidence. Uncertainty and anxiety can be expected in the early stages of the information search process. The affective symptoms of uncertainty, confusion, and frustration are associated with vague, unclear thoughts about a topic or question. As knowledge states shift to more clearly focused thoughts, a parallel shift occurs in feelings of increased confidence.

The emotional state described in the uncertainty principle is captured by the reflections the following first-term MA students[1] make on their information searching experiences:

> Student A: '[...] sometimes I get desperate when I cannot find any information at all [...]'

> Student B: 'The difficult thing is to find just what you need, and not thousands of articles about completely irrelevant stuff.'

Kuhlthau points out that uncertainty is the very trigger for initiating the information searching process and thus the research process. Uncertainty is admittedly part and parcel of the research process, but if it becomes too dominant, it might lead to writer's block and, in the long run, hinder academic progress. Handling uncertainty may be even a greater challenge for postgraduate students in the humanities, as they may easily feel psychologically and physically isolated when working.

In the next section, a number of research supervision models are discussed. New insights are given into what kind of supervision the librarian should pursue to support the student in the light of the needs and challenges just described.

Intervening in the student's research process: a discussion of supervision models for the academic librarian

As Handal and Lauvås (2006, p. 53) point out, supervision should be a flexible activity. Every student is different and her situation varies throughout the research process. Therefore, the supervisor should have a set of strategies and methods to choose from. From the librarian's perspective, traditional source-oriented supervision may be very useful at the later stages of the information searching process, but other stages will require other supervision strategies and methods. Handal and Lauvås highlight the importance of changing supervision style in accordance with where the student is in the research process. Throughout this process, the librarian should be able to play a *multiplicity* of roles, each of them characterised by different supervisory strategies. In this way, the librarian will be able to design a model of supervision that caters for the student's needs in the different research phases.

The academic librarian as a counsellor

Source-oriented intervention in the user's information searching has been traditionally dominant in the academic library. The academic librarian has focused on library resources and on locating information in her individual supervision and group instruction. Much attention has been devoted to all details regarding the functionality of any given database, such as how to truncate or how to narrow down a long hit list (see Scenario 4.1, p. 86). Instruction and supervision have been of the 'one size fits all' kind.

In her discussion of librarian contact with users, Kuhlthau (2004, pp. 116–126) argues that intervention within the bibliographic paradigm, i.e. advice and assistance that is source-oriented rather than process-oriented, is of limited value. In source-oriented intervention, it is assumed that there is a right answer and a right single source or group of sources matching the student's question. There is no real accommodation to the student's specific information needs. The information is identified 'without consideration for the users' particular point of view, level of knowledge, or stage in the search process. [...] Users are assumed to approach problems from a uniform perspective, knowledge state, and stage of process' (*ibid.*, p. 117).

Admittedly, source-oriented supervision may be valuable and effective at later stages of the searching process, when users have a clear task focus and thus can articulate their information needs in a specific way. However, this kind of intervention is not likely to match the student's information needs at the early stages of the information searching process. Then the student's cognitive state of mind is characterised by uncertainty and vagueness. Kuhlthau reports that students can easily experience information overload, more uncertainty and confusion, and even writing blocks, if source-oriented intervention takes place at the wrong stage of process.

Kuhlthau (2004) argues for librarian intervention into the process of the user that she labels as a *counsellor* role. In her view, this is the kind of intervention that really facilitates the student's searching and thus research process in our technological information age. The student learns from information in a constructive process. Her research question develops and the librarian's supervisory role accommodates this gradual development. The search process is 'highly individual, creative, and personal' (*ibid.*, p. 119). The student and the librarian have a dialogue over time that focuses on the student's specific research question. Through this dialogue, the librarian can assist the student in her redefinition of the research question, choice of a search strategy, and identification of appropriate sources at the different stages of her (re)search process. The librarian, like the academic supervisor, can help the student by guiding her through the creative process of constructing meaning, that is, of seeking certainty and clarity in her academic work.

In practical terms, the counsellor role entails a supervision style that is not controlling, i.e. that does not impose specific advice, ideas, or suggestions on the student. The drawback of controlling supervision is that it may easily result in the supervisor doing the thinking and finding solutions on behalf of the student. In less controlling supervision, the supervisor is a 'writing coach' (Dysthe *et al.* 2000, p.170, based on Clark and Fry, 1992). Following this model, communication between the librarian and the student can be characterised as follows:

- The student talks, the librarian listens, asks questions, and gives positive feedback.
- The student decides on what the supervision session will be about.
- The librarian encourages the student to express her own thoughts, problems, and alternatives.
- The librarian formulates ideas, suggestions, and advice as questions.

- The librarian does not interrupt the student to impose her own ideas.

- The librarian takes notes or records the session, and gives the student the notes or recording after the session.

Dysthe *et al.* (2000, pp. 169–170) emphasise the use of questions as a central supervision strategy. They give the following as an example:

- How would you describe the problem?

- Have you got any ideas as to how to proceed now?

- What do you think about this question?

- Which of the solutions seems to be best?

- What happens if you go for this alternative?

Dysthe *et al.* argue that posing questions helps the student make progress in her idea development. They encourage the student to take responsibility for finding solutions and answers. Questions and unresolved problems keep us thinking and wondering, both at a conscious and unconscious level. Through the use of questions like these, the librarian becomes a problem *spotter*, rather than a problem *solver*.

To conclude, we propose a model of librarian intervention in the student's research process that goes beyond the location of information. Giving student physical/electronic access to information does not guarantee that they become informed. Access to information does not necessarily result in knowledge. Instead, the librarian's intervention should help students gain 'intellectual access' (Buckland, 1991) to information. By acting as a counsellor, the librarian adopts a supervision strategy based on asking questions and identifying problems. This supervision style fosters librarian intervention in the student's seeking meaning and gaining knowledge, in her interpretation and use of information for thinking and learning. In Kuhlthau's (2004) view, these are central issues at the heart of information literacy education.

The academic librarian as a process-oriented supervisor

Professionalising the role of academic librarians requires some formalisation of the relationship between the academic librarian and the academic supervisor in relation to student supervision. The question 'who does what and what should we do together?' must be addressed for the sake of each of the parties in the supervision process schematised in Figure 4.1.

One way of describing the relationship between academic supervisor and academic librarian is to assign the former the role of *primary* supervisor, and of *secondary* supervisor to the latter. The primary supervisor has overall responsibility, whereas the secondary supervisor plays a complementary role (Handal and Lauvås, 2006, pp. 215–216). Nevertheless, the secondary supervisor has formal status. She is a resource person or special consultant who offers advice and assistance in her particular area of expertise. The academic librarian fits into this secondary role, as an expert in matters concerning information search and exploitation as well as having academic qualifications in a certain discipline.

Figure 4.1   Parties in the individual student supervision process

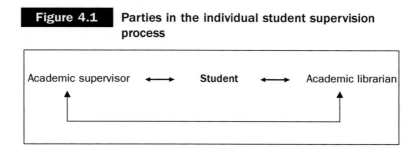

Process supervision

The relationship between the librarian's and the academic supervisor's roles can be further explored through the distinction between *process* and *product* supervision proposed by Handal and Lauvås (based on Lindén, 1998). The student's research process can be facilitated if the academic librarian's supervision is mainly understood as *process* supervision. By contrast, the academic supervisor will alternate between process and product supervision. As a process supervisor, the librarian:

- guides and encourages the student to move on in her developing research process over time, especially in matters related to information search and use;
- does not focus on the final thesis or drafts and their quality, unlike the product-oriented supervisor;
- contributes to the student's development of a professional identity as a researcher, for instance, as regards professional ethics in using information in research work.

In what follows, we elaborate upon the role of the librarian as a process-oriented supervisor. We do so by characterising her intervention in the students' writing process. In the process supervision described here, there is likely to be some overlap between the intervention of the academic supervisor and the academic librarian in the student's writing process. The librarian, the academic supervisor, and the supervisee should negotiate locally how this overlap will be handled, both at the beginning of the supervisee's research process and along the way. Nevertheless, here we suggest a few guidelines on how process supervision may proceed in general.

If the librarian is not to assess the student's final product, process supervision seems appropriate for a number of reasons. Handal and Lauvås (2006, p. 60) claim that process supervision is valuable at the initial stages of the research process, especially when students feel uncertainty. At the early stages, narrowing down a research question from the chosen general topic is not an easy task for the student, as pointed out in the section on 'Student needs and challenges' (see p. 69). Obtaining a reasonable overview of the literature on a given topic in Kuhlthau's pre-focus exploration phase (See Table 4.2) is not a simple task either, given the vast amount of information the student has access to nowadays. For this reason, we believe that students can also benefit from the academic librarian's process supervision at the early stages.

Texts for thinking

As a process-oriented supervisor, the librarian can focus her intervention on the student's writing 'for thinking' (Dysthe *et al.*, 2000). By contrast, the academic supervisor will follow up both the student's writing 'for thinking' and 'for presentation' (*ibid.*). The distinction between these two types of writing was introduced in 'The writing process' (see p. 67). Writing for thinking focuses on process and not on a final text that will be assessed. It is writing for learning.

The librarian can support the student by encouraging her to produce different types of texts for thinking from day 1, for example brainstorming, mindmapping, first notes. Dysthe *et al.* agree that 'writing for thinking' will be most fruitful in the creative phases of the writing process. In Kuhlthau's topic selection and pre-focus exploration, uncensored writing will help creative development and will support the student's exploration of concepts and ideas. The student need not worry about formal requirements, the quality of her texts or the product supervisor's censoring hand. The texts the librarian may be presented with should be regarded as the basis for process supervision. They are tools to assess where the student is in the research process and to enable her to move on to the next phase in her searching and writing. Dysthe *et al.* argue that writing for thinking is valuable in that it forces students to clarify the very ideas that they will need to communicate to others at a later stage. This will avoid lack of clarity and ambiguity in their text due to poor understanding of the research problem or poor formulation of their thoughts.

Texts for thinking will guide the student in her searching process, and by the same token, the searching will help the student narrow down her research topic and make headway in her writing. Understanding the literature through writing for thinking will help students transform the information they have read into their own knowledge in the context of the research question. In individual supervision, the process-oriented librarian can be a 'listening partner', who, with the help of the student's texts for thinking, can help her in narrowing down the research topic and formulating a research question. By talking aloud about her research topic and plans, the student might be in a better position to confront the feelings of uncertainty and anxiety at the beginning. In addition, if the librarian encourages a metadiscussion of these feelings, this might help the student to come to terms with them and accept them as a part and parcel of the research process she is embarking on. Scenario 4.4 (see pp. 88–89) illustrates how process supervision can proceed in practice.

Handal and Lauvås (2006) argue that supervisors should alternate between process- and product-oriented supervision depending on the students' needs at each point in time. For instance, in more critical phases of the writing process, 'writing for presentation' will be central and this writing will call for product-oriented supervision. Texts will need to be rewritten and edited in order for others (e.g. classmates, examiner, supervisor) to be able to understand them. Such textual needs may arise especially in the writing that takes place throughout Kuhlthau's phases focus formulation, information collection and search closure. Nevertheless, in the case of the academic librarian, we would like to stress that supervision should be mainly process-oriented. For the aim is to guide the student in her (re)search process and there is no formal involvement in the student's final assessment. An exception to this is possibly what Handal and Lauvås characterise as *ad hoc* supervision. This is problem-solving supervision that academic librarians are very used to. *Ad hoc* supervision has elements of both source and product-oriented supervision. The student contacts the librarian when she experiences a specific problem in her work. The student can make an appointment (e.g. through a 'book-a-librarian' service) or simply knock on the librarian's door. For instance, the student may want to check with the librarian whether particular instances of referencing are correct. She may likewise seek help if she does not succeed in finding pertinent literature in the library journal databases. It is important for the academic librarian to try to contextualise the student's needs at that point within the totality of her research process so as to avoid ineffective 'one size fits all' assistance.

Conclusions

To conclude, extending the role of the academic librarian as a supervisor requires defining on what kind of partnership the librarian, the academic supervisor, and the student are embarking. It also calls for a reflection on the librarian's part on the multiplicity of supervisory roles that the student's research process demands. Not doing this reflection work can have unfortunate consequences. The student might receive conflicting feedback from the supervisor and academic librarian that might confuse her and hinder her progress. Both library and faculty staff might feel that librarians are suddenly treading on 'faculty territory'. Further, the librarian might fear that she is not competent enough to do the supervisory job. Ideally, metacommunication about supervision, as described by Handal and Lauvås (2006), should include a third party, namely the academic librarian, from as early as possible in the student's research process. Explicitly discussing supervision expectations, duties and strategies with both the student and the academic supervisor will help the librarian delimit her supervisory role in a way that satisfies all three parties. In the next section, we move on to explore group supervision at the academic library.

Learning as a social practice: masters and apprentices at the academic library

Kvale (1997) puts forth research apprenticeship as a possible model to organise research education. He argues that research apprenticeship is significant for learning in academia. Inspired by Lave and Wenger's (1991) theory of learning as social practice, Kvale discusses four key aspects of apprenticeship:

- Participating in communities of practice
- Acquiring a professional identity
- Learning by doing
- Evaluation through practice.

These aspects can be applied to the training of researchers in order to facilitate the acquisition of complex intellectual skills. At the end of his article, Kvale (1997, p. 193) makes a call for further investigation of 'the educational potentials of apprenticeship', among other things, 'as an incitement to understand and develop the potentials of human learning as a social practice'. In what follows, apprenticeship is discussed as a possible model for library user education and supervision.

The academic library as a learning centre should promote learning as a social practice by designing supervision that enhances the apprenticeship aspects highlighted by Kvale. Apprenticeship can strengthen the focus on the student and her research process. In a similar way to Kvale's argument for apprenticeship in other academic settings, apprenticeship at the library can facilitate the acquisition of information literacy skills (e.g. critical evaluation of sources, ethic use of sources, literature search), as part of the complex intellectual skills Kvale refers to. If information search and use are looked upon as activities in the research process, we can draw similarities between those activities and what Kvale calls 'research as craft' (1997, p. 190). Apprenticeship and learning as a social practice can be enhanced through library workshops where the overall learning goal is for students to become information literate.

Hands-on workshops like the one illustrated in Scenario 4.2 (see pp. 86–87) give students the chance to participate in a community of practice. Samara (2006) discusses the rewards of organised student support. Her research on study groups ('skrivegrupper') reveals that they help the student progress in her work as well as increasing her motivation and self-confidence. Furthermore, organised support gives the student the chance to become socialised into her discipline. The group gives a sense of community and diminishes the feeling of isolation mentioned in the section on 'Student needs and challenges' (see p. 69). Although Samara's study concentrates on study groups, library workshops that are based on her study group model may have similar positive effects on the student. Whether focusing on writing or on information searching and use, organised support initiatives such as workshops will assist the student both academically and psychologically. A discussion of library workshops based on Samara's study group model is, however, beyond the scope of this book.

In the workshops, the information professional should be a *coach* (Kvale, 1997), rather than exclusively playing the *teacher* role of both the transmission model of supervision (Dysthe, 2006, pp. 233–235) and the bibliographic paradigm of library education (see the section on 'The academic librarian as a counsellor', pp. 72–75). Just as students 'learn science by doing science' (Kvale, 1997, p. 190), they can acquire information literacy by doing information literacy related activities. These activities should be based on the student's specific work. In this way, her research process can benefit from her dialogue with the librarian and her fellow students as well as their feedback.

Students learn a lot from each other through their interaction and dialogue (Lave and Wenger, 1991; Samara, 2006). In the workshops, they can progress in their research process through *scaffolding* (Wood *et al.*, 1976). In scaffolding, the supervisor helps the student master new knowledge and skills by explicitly discussing and showing new actions that the student can make her own and practise alone later on (Handal and Lauvås, 2006, p. 57). Scaffolding can be further encouraged by asking students to work with others and to provide feedback on each other's information work at hand (see Scenario 4.2, pp. 86–87). Students who are more advanced can be coaches for those who are at more initial research stages. The workshops will also give students the chance to evaluate their information practices with both the information professional and their fellow students.

One of the goals of postgraduate education is socialisation into the academic culture (Dysthe *et al.*, 2006). Group supervision in library workshops can be seen as essentially complementing individual supervision. Individual supervision alone does not enable the student to learn the knowledge and skills she should have as a legitimate member of the research community. In short, library workshops can constitute a learning space where students experience the plurality of voices that Dysthe *et al.* (2006) argue for. Dialogue is an essential component in the apprenticeship model, where knowledge is constructed through the interaction between different parties and voices (Dysthe, 2006). Kuhlthau (2004) also singles out dialogue as a key component in process-oriented individual supervision. Likewise, successful group supervision in workshops is dependent on dialogue. The use of student's texts such as preliminary formulations of a research question, first notes, and mindmapping can serve a dialogical function. They can be tools that engage the students and the information professional in a dialogical process (Dysthe, 2006) by encouraging them to listen and to think aloud. From this dialogic perspective, supervision is a social process that involves more partners than the traditional supervisor–supervisee relationship. Figure 4.2 schematises the interacting parties in supervision as a whole.

Finally, library workshops can help the student to reinforce her professional identity in terms of how researchers find and exploit information in an effective, creative, and ethical way. The apprenticeship model applied to library supervision will help the student to gradually become a legitimate member of the research community, as well as preparing her for lifelong

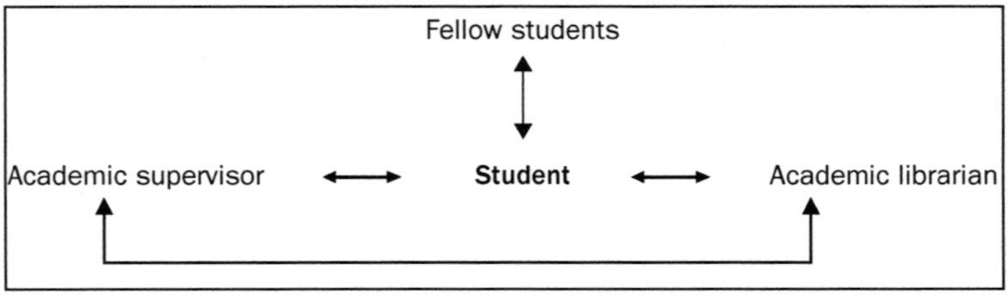

Figure 4.2   Parties in the supervision process as a whole

learning. In the next section, a number of scenarios are presented to illustrate how the supervision models just discussed can be applied to library user education and supervision.

Process-oriented library supervision: a discussion of scenarios

This section aims at elaborating on the academic librarian's supervisory role in practice through the presentation and discussion of four scenarios. In a librarian training situation, these scenarios can be used as materials for a metadiscussion of the librarian's role as a supervisor. The scenarios have been inspired by our supervising and teaching experience at the academic library. Scenarios 4.1 and 4.2 illustrate group supervision, whereas 4.3 and 4.4 give instances of individual supervision. All the scenarios concentrate on the initial stage of the research process. Handal and Lauvås (2006) highlight the importance of individual supervision at this stage. Likewise, Cavallin (2006) stresses the relevance of group supervision at the initial stage. The group supports the student psychologically by offering her a sense of community and of sharing similar challenges. On the other hand, group supervision helps the student choose and narrow down a topic, as well as formulating a preliminary research question. In our opinion, library supervision, whether individual or in groups, can serve a similar key function at the task initiation and pre-focus exploration stages (Kuhlthau, 2004). In addition to helping the student get started on her research process and promote learning in a social context, it can also help her come to terms with uncertainty and anxiety. Scenarios 4.1 and 4.2 contrast source-oriented and process-oriented teaching and supervision.

Scenario 4.1

Lena is a senior academic librarian at a university library. Today she is teaching a 2-hour course in literature searching for thesis writing. There are eight MA linguistics students attending her course. Their lecturer has informed Lena that they are all starting their MA thesis this semester and writing on topics related to language acquisition.

Lena has divided her session into two parts. In the first part, she goes through the library journal databases and e-bibliographies relevant to linguistics. She assumes that the students master the OPAC, as this is content covered by user education at BA level. Thus she skips the OPAC in her demonstration and takes up MLA, ISI Web of Science, PsycINFO, Bibliographie Linguistique and Linguistics Abstracts Online. She describes each database and shows its main functionalities. She conducts a search example and explains the search result. In the second part, students are asked to do a number of searching exercises she has designed so that they become familiar with the databases. To make the exercises more relevant to the students, they all relate to searching literature on language acquisition.

The demonstration part of the course has taken longer time than planned and, as a result, they only have time to discuss the answer to a few exercises. However, being an experienced library instructor, Lena has already prepared a key to the exercises, which she hands out to the students at the end of the session.

Scenario 4.2

An academic librarian, Paul, is giving a workshop in advanced literature searching for a small group of Spanish language MA students. They are now working on their research statement. Their current research question, which they have e-mailed Paul in advance, and a short debriefing show that they are at slightly different stages. Whereas some have started searching in the OPAC and Google, others have not because they still feel confused and vague about their topic.

First, the workshop focuses on preparing for one's literature search. Each student writes down their topic/research question and gives it to the student sitting next to her. Each student is asked to provide a list of keywords with synonyms for their fellow student's research question. Based on these written activities, students discuss their own research questions and refine their keyword list in dialogue with others. Subsequently, Paul initiates a whole group discussion on which library databases may be relevant at initial and more advanced search stages. For instance, the OPAC is classed as a good starting point to find introductions and textbooks on one's general topic.

Finally, students are asked to search in the databases they find relevant using their keyword lists and combinations. Students working on similar topics are encouraged to sit together. All along, Paul tries to fade into the background while surveying the students' searching activities and discussion. He goes around and intervenes when students run into problems. When questions arise that may benefit the entire group, he tries to elicit answers from the class and provides explanations and reflections. At the end of the workshop, each student reports on their searching experience to the rest of the group, for example on difficulties experienced, good search tips, hit lists, and further searching plans.

In Scenario 4.1, Lena embodies the bibliographic instruction paradigm and the transmission model of education. Her focus is on library resources and on providing the right answer. She assumes student's needs and designs her course independently of their views, knowledge, and stage of process. Dialogue does not really have a place in her course. The writing that she encourages is of little relevance to the student's specific research process. By contrast, in Scenario 4.2,

Paul embodies Kuhlthau's *counsellor*, the process supervisor and Kvale's *coach*. Dialogue and writing are central elements in a session where master and apprentices work together. Students are invited to learn from each other and to take responsibility for their own learning. The focus is on the student's needs and work.

Individual supervision in Scenarios 4.3 and 4.4 further illustrate intervention within the bibliographic instruction and the process paradigms respectively.

Scenario 4.3

An academic librarian, Matilda, is working at the reference desk today. A student comes up to her and asks for help to find literature. Matilda does her best to find out what the student wants to write about, but she only seems to obtain vague answers from the student. It looks like this student is interested in equal opportunities and ethnic minorities, but in Matilda's opinion, she is nowhere near a preliminary research question. She is a typical case of confused MA student trying to write her research statement.

Matilda conducts a search in the library catalogue that gives about 800 hits. The student looks increasingly stressed, and Matilda does not want her to drown in a sea of references. She thus tells the student to forget about the piles of sources in the library at this point. She advises her to think about her topic a bit more and to come back to the library, once she has managed to narrow her topic down.

(*Source*: adapted from Torras and Skagen, 2007)

Scenario 4.4

Mark is planning to write his MA thesis on multicultural communication in health services. He works in a hospital, where he hopes to obtain his data. His research statement

---

is due soon, and he feels at a loss as to how to formulate his topic. He could do with an appointment with his supervisor, but he does not want to make a fool of himself or waste his precious supervision time. Reading should definitely give him some inspiration, but he does not know where to start.

Following a fellow student's advice, he has made an appointment with Esther, a subject specialist at the library. Esther asks him to tell her all about his research topic. Mark feels unable to articulate a single thought. Nevertheless, after a while, they succeed in doing some brainstorming on possible topics, theoretical approaches, data collection methodologies, and research ethical issues. As they are talking, Esther suggests that Mark should write down a list of key concepts and ideas, which he can use later to write a summary of their discussion. Mark can use this summary to start working on his research statement and to prepare for his literature searching.

They conclude that what Mark needs now is an overview of the literature on his topic so that he can start writing his literature review. Esther invites Mark to sit at her computer and start a preliminary search using his key concepts. Mark finds some interesting books in the OPAC. He seems quite determined to use critical discourse analysis as his theoretical framework, as his supervisor is an authority in this area. Esther is critical of this theoretical approach. However, she limits herself to helping Mark find some introductory books on multicultural communication and on health service communication from this theoretical perspective. At the end of their meeting, Esther and Mark agree to meet later on again, when Mark feels the need for more specific literature.

Matilda and Lena are information gatekeepers. They own the knowledge and their intervention is based on right answers to right queries. The focus is not on meeting student needs, but on locating the right sources. Matilda looks upon herself as an information *identifier* (Kuhlthau, 2004, p. 117). As the student does not have a satisfactory research question, she cannot provide a satisfactory list of resources and thus decides not to intervene. She seems to be aware of the student's difficulty and uncertainty and recognises the dangers of information overload, but she does not have a role to play at this initial stage. Matilda is product-oriented. Collecting the right sources is all the student needs to achieve understanding. Exploring and formulating tentative research questions are not seen as issues on which student and librarian interaction can be based. When the student is sent away, one wonders whether Matilda's presumed lack of intervention might actually have a negative effect on the student's research process. The experience might actually have increased her feelings of uncertainty and isolation along the lines described in the section on 'Student needs and challenges' (see p. 69). The task of formulating a research question and reading about the topic might now seem more insurmountable than ever.

Scenario 4.4 describes quite a different supervision situation. Like Paul, Esther intervenes in the student's process. The student's needs matter. She coaches Mark in his process of narrowing down a topic. Their interaction is based on dialogue and writing. Process-oriented supervision naturally leads to a number of encounters, which Esther is aware of. Other supervisory roles might be relevant later on. An *identifier* role à la Matilda may be necessary when Mark has a very clear focus and a good overview of his topic, and needs very specific literature (Kuhlthau's 'information collection' stage). Likewise Mark will benefit from product supervision, if he takes up referencing questions with Esther (e.g. at Kuhlthau's 'information collection' and 'search closure' stages).

It is interesting to note Esther's behaviour regarding Mark's choice of theoretical approach. Although she could have argued against his choice, her intervention has a limit.

Mark is responsible for his own research process and, on the other hand, he cannot be placed in a position where he receives conflicting feedback from his librarian and his academic supervisor. Esther is a secondary supervisor.

To conclude, the scenarios just presented can be useful discussion triggers in librarian training. By analysing the attitudes, assumptions, and expectations that these four scenarios portray in terms of the librarian's role in the student's research process, information professionals can reflect on their work and on the intervention they should have. As Dysthe (2006) points out, a discussion of potential supervisory roles will increase the professional's awareness of own practice as well as improving it to support the student's research process better.

Conclusions

A large number of academic libraries around the world are experiencing the need for professional development in their aim to become learning centres on a par with other higher education institutions. This chapter has characterised the information professional's extended role as a supervisor at the academic library. The postgraduate students' information needs and challenges have been discussed, on the basis of research on academic writing and information searching behaviour. Subsequently, the discussion has concentrated on how the academic librarian can best support the student's research process. An attempt has been made to apply a number of research supervision models to the academic library context. To sum up, academic librarians should aim at a model of supervision with the following characteristics:

- Group and individual supervision are contextualised and process-oriented, i.e. they focus on the student's specific needs, state of knowledge, and stage throughout the research process. Nevertheless, the librarian should be flexible and ready to adopt a multiplicity of supervisory roles. There might be a need for switching into product supervision and identifier roles.

- Supervision focuses on the interpretation and use of information for thinking and learning.

- Supervision is based on dialogue between the student and her peers and between the student, the academic supervisor, and the librarian.

- Supervision encourages the production of different text types from day 1.

- It gives students the chance to participate in workshops that function as communities of practice. The workshops promote learning by doing and scaffolding, metadiscussion of research activities, and psychological states as well as evaluation of own practice.

- Supervision takes into account psychological factors by making it possible for the student to learn strategies and skills to tackle uncertainty and anxiety. It further gives the student a sense of community through workshop participation.

- The definition of specific supervision tasks and responsibilities is subject to explicit discussion between the student, the librarian, and the academic supervisor.

Adopting the model of supervision just outlined is not challenge free. In process supervision, the supervisor follows up and coaches the student in her research. This entails several meetings throughout the process. As Handal and Lauvås (2006) note, the student and the academic supervisor embark on a fairly long collaboration and develop a relatively close relationship. The relationship between the academic librarian and the student cannot be characterised in the same way. Traditionally, the contact between them has been limited to one or two library courses per semester and possibly some *ad hoc* supervision.

Another challenge is succeeding in making library-organised support relevant to the student. In many universities, library workshops are not compulsory, and thus low student attendance is not unusual. On the other hand, postgraduate students in the humanities and social sciences are not used to group supervision. There is a dominant individualistic tradition (Lee, 1998, quoted in Dysthe *et al.*, 2006, p. 49). The postgraduate student devotes all her time and effort on her thesis. Workshops like the one in Scenario 4.2 may thus be experienced as a waste of time, and the student may choose to resort to *ad hoc* supervision instead.

The academic supervisor and the academic librarian need to define how their tandem is to share the supervisory role in practice. This will require some discussion and negotiation, which may not always be a straightforward task. The student research process, as described in Tables 4.1 and 4.2 above, and the students' difficulties and challenges outlined in the section on 'Student needs and challenges' (see p. 69) may prove to be valuable discussion topics to initiate the collaborative work. The library and the faculty have traditionally led separate lives. Neither the librarian nor the academic supervisor may be fully aware of the pedagogical potential of university libraries. Academic libraries will benefit from making specific plans of action both for marketing themselves as teaching institutions and for ensuring adequate professional development of their staff. Librarians' pedagogical competence and supervisory skills can be improved through in-house training in specific issues such as designing teaching materials, course evaluation, and teaching methodology. Librarians may also want to consider participating in the teacher training modules that many universities offer to the academic staff.

Closer collaboration between the faculty and library is mandatory in order to implement a process-oriented model of supervision at the library. In terms of library group supervision, academic librarians and academic staff also need to collaborate to incorporate library supervision and user education in the curricula. Incorporation will involve some administrative cost, which may be felt as a resource problem.

Finally, despite the challenges, including the academic librarian in the supervision constellation will reward all its parties. Students will be supported better in their research process, and their acquisition of complex intellectual skills will be more comprehensive. In sharing supervision with the academic librarian, the academic supervisor will be partially or even totally relieved of some tasks. For instance, outsourcing citation or basic critical evaluation of information to the library will spare the academic staff some precious supervision and teaching time. In addition, it will clarify expectations in terms of student work quality. For the academic librarian, a more active participation in the faculty's research activities through supervision will result in more adequate user education and contact with users. The librarian will also gain more insight into collection development needs, as she will be more aware of the faculty's research areas. Last but not least, including the academic librarian in the supervision constellation will contribute to the professionalisation of her educational role.

Note

1. These reflections were obtained through a written evaluation form after a course in advanced literature searching for MA students.

5

Conclusions

This book has presented a process-oriented approach to information literacy education for the academic library. Our ideas and suggestions are grounded in a didactic approach to user education. Our approach to user education is further underpinned by a socio-cultural perspective on knowledge, whereby learning is regarded as a social phenomenon. This view is particularly highlighted in our model of library supervision, which promotes dialogue between all stakeholders in supervision, as well as participation in communities of practice. Our approach to user education both challenges and enables practitioners to reflect on the values, theoretical foundations, and experience-based background underlying their practice. It also provides them with pedagogical tools to facilitate her work on planning and carrying out information literacy courses, as well as supervising students in their research process.

Adopting a didactic approach to information literacy education is an essential condition for professionalising the educational role of the library practitioner. Professionalisation of the educational role of the information professional is a key factor to give the academic library the status of the formal learning arena it struggles to attain. At the individual level we have presented the library practitioner as a professional and autonomous educator. As such, she is capable of making theoretically founded and independent choices and decisions in her teaching and supervising practice. Likewise, she is willing and capable of assessing her educational practice critically. She can also analyse the relationship between education theory, curriculum planning, and daily practice critically. At the organisational level, we have highlighted the need for library management and library staff to collaborate closely in order to lay the theoretical foundations of an information literacy programme. The application of the *theoretical triangle of practice* and the *didactic relation model* to library user education intend to facilitate these individual and collective tasks.

In its development work, the academic library needs to look to the future: What will its users be like? And how can user education be tailored to their searching behaviour? The report commissioned by The British Library and JSIC (2008), *Information behaviour of the researcher of the future*, raises concerns about how prepared the academic library is to empower future researchers. The report characterises the Google generation, born after 1993, as being unaware of library-sponsored content or at least reluctant to use it. It also reports on how less keen this generation is on using the physical library to find relevant information. It resorts to internet searching engines instead. Further, this generation is little concerned with authority, shows little respect of copyright, and their academic work raises serious plagiarism issues. We hope that the approach to user education in this book will provide information professionals with a framework within which they can start anticipating the future today.

At its heart this book advocates for the academic library as a *learning organisation*, which is a vision shared by increasingly more educational institutions (Cavaleri and Fearon, 1996). Moving away from the transmission model of user education makes the information professional a facilitator of learning rather than a sheer provider of information or information gatekeeper. She thus faces the challenge of shifting from the safe role of bibliographic instructor to that of *information empowerment specialist* (White, 1992). Empowerment is understood here as the development of knowledge, skills, and abilities in the students to enable them to control and develop their own learning (Harvey, 2004). Nevertheless, we believe that no student empowerment can take place through information literacy education without information professional empowerment.

As in all learning organisations, empowerment is dependent on the staff's engagement in 'transformational learning and change' (Lander, 2004). Further, the empowerment of the library practitioner requires a total change of attitude from all the parties involved and a willingness to empower and to be empowered (Fourie, 1999, p. 383). Among other things, this means that the library staff must embrace its commitment to information literacy. In our knowledge-based economy, highly skilled workforce is required to have the capacity to learn continuously (Andretta, 2005a,b) and this is what information literacy education promotes. The staff must endorse the view that information literacy is a means of individual empowerment in today's information society.

New professional roles call for new competencies. In this sense, the library, understood as a learning organisation, can provide the information professional with the necessary support and development to adapt to a rapidly changing information environment. The library should give room for professional development and knowledge dissemination in daily educational tasks. Just as importantly, it should rationalise available resources to advance development and cater for new tasks. Team work is an optimal organisation model to ensure that competencies and knowledge are shared and developed by the whole library staff as a learning community of practice. A condition for success is the library's ability to continuously reflect on and evaluate its goals and lines of action. The approach to user education proposed in this book is meant to foster an educational platform for information literacy upon which library performance can be improved and continuous learning and development facilitated.

Appendix 1:
Course evaluation form

In order to improve our courses, we would like you to know what you think about the course you have just taken.

Please answer the questions below as fully as possible and tick off a number between 1 and 5 to evaluate the course.

1. What were your expectations about this course?

2. Has it lived up to your expectations?

3. Have you taken other courses offered by this library? If so, which?

4. Did you find the course relevant?
    Very relevant 1 ☐ 2 ☐ 3 ☐ 4 ☐ 5 ☐ Not relevant
    Please justify your answer.

5. The course learning goals were made clear.
    Strongly agree 1 ☐ 2 ☐ 3 ☐ 4 ☐ 5 ☐ Strongly disagree

6. The presentation of the materials was clear and well structured.
    Strongly agree 1 ☐ 2 ☐ 3 ☐ 4 ☐ 5 ☐ Strongly disagree

7. It was possible to ask and discuss questions during the course.

    Strongly agree 1 ☐ 2 ☐ 3 ☐ 4 ☐ 5 ☐ Strongly disagree

8. There was enough time to do the course activities.

    Strongly agree 1 ☐ 2 ☐ 3 ☐ 4 ☐ 5 ☐ Strongly disagree

9. I was able to keep pace with the course.

    Strongly agree 1 ☐ 2 ☐ 3 ☐ 4 ☐ 5 ☐ Strongly disagree

10. How could the course have been improved?

(*Source*: Excerpt of evaluation form used at the University of Bergen library.)

References

Aalborg University Library (2006) *SWIM2 English version. The concept* (Internet), Aalborg University Library, Denmark. Available from: http://www.learningobjects web.dk/pdf/The%20SWIM2%20concept.pdf (Accessed 16 November 2007).

Andretta, S. (2005a) *Information literacy: a practitioner's guide.* Oxford, Chandos.

Andretta, S. (2005b) *Information literacy: empowering the learner 'against all odds'* (Internet), paper presented at the Librarians' Information Literacy Annual Conference (LILAC), 4–6 April 2005, Imperial College, London UK. Available from: http://www.cilip.org.uk/NR/rdonlyres/ FD11F35B-69DF-41D9-B0E1–38DC47BA6FEB/0/ andretta.pdf (Accessed 15 February 2008).

Andretta, S. (2007) Editorial. Information literacy: the functional literacy for the 21st century. In: Andretta, S. ed. *Change and challenge. Information literacy for the 21st century.* Adelaida, Auslib Press, pp. 1–13.

Bergen University College (2007) *Kunnskap til yrke. Strategisk plan for Høgskolen i Bergen 2005–2010* (Internet), Bergen, Bergen University College. Available from: http://www .hib.no/om/sentrale%2Ddokumenter/strategi-og-planer/ strategisk_plan/index.htm (Accessed 2 February 2008).

Bergen University College Library (2008) *Ledetråder i åpent læringslandskap. Pedagogisk grunnlagsdokument for HiB – bibliotekets opplæring i søk og bruk av informasjonskilder.* Bergen, Bergen University College

Library. Available from: http://www.hib.no/biblioteket/ strategiskplan/documents/Ledertraderiapentlaeringslan dskap2008.doc (Accessed 15 July 2008).

Bjørndal, B. and Lieberg, S. (1978) *Nye veier i didaktikken? En innføring i didaktiske emner og begreper.* Oslo, Aschehoug and Co.

Blaabjerg, N.J. (2005) User centred information literacy education – application of multimedia in e-learning and blended learning. In: *Proceedings of the 3rd international conference on education and information systems: Technologies and applications* (Internet), vol. II, Orlando, Florida, USA, pp. 152–155. Available from: http://www .swiminfo.dk/pdf/EISTA05_E721YC.pdf (Accessed 10 November 2007).

Bråten, I. (2002) Selvregulert læring i sosialt-kognitiv perspektiv. In: Bråten, I. ed. *Læring i sosialt, kognitivt og sosialt-kognitivt perspektiv.* Oslo, Cappelens Forlag, pp. 164–193.

Buckland, M. (1991) *Information and information systems.* New York, Greenwood Press.

Bundy, A. ed. (2004) *Australian and New Zealand information literacy framework. Principles, standards and practice.* 2nd edition (Internet), Adelaide, Australian and New Zealand Institute for Information Literacy. Available from: http://www.anziil.org/resources/Info% 20lit%202nd%20edition.pdf (Accessed 11 February 2008).

Carroll, J. (2002) *A handbook for deterring plagiarism in higher education.* Oxford, Oxford Centre for Staff and Learning Development.

Cavaleri, S. and Fearon, D. eds. (1996) *Managing in organizations that learn.* Oxford, Blackwell.

Cavallin, C. (2006) Gruppebasert veiledning med én veileder i masterstudier. In: Dysthe, O. and Samara, A. eds. *Forskningsveiledning på master- og doktorgradsnivå.* Oslo, Abstrakt forlag, pp. 56–64.

Chartered Institute of Library and Information Professionals (CILIP) (2005) Defining Information Literacy for the UK. *Update Magazine* (Internet), January/February. Information Literacy Group. Available from: http://www .cilip.org.uk/publications/updatemagazine/archive/archive 2005/janfeb/armstrong.htm (Accessed 17 July 2007).

Clark, R.P. and Fry, D. (1992) *Coaching writers. Editors and reporters working together.* New York, St Martin's Press. Quoted in: Dysthe, O., Hertzberg, F. and Hoel, T.L. (2000) *Skrive for å lære. Skriving i høyere utdanning.* Oslo, Abstrakt forlag, p. 170.

Dewey, J. (1963) *Experience and education.* London, Collier-Macmillan.

Dysthe, O. (2001) Sosiokulturelle teoriperspektiv på kunnskap og læring. In: Dysthe, O. ed. *Dialog, samspel og læring.* Oslo, Abstrakt forlag, pp. 33–72.

Dysthe, O. (2006) Rettleiaren som lærar, partnar eller meister?. In: Dysthe, O. and Samara, A. eds. *Forskningsveiledning på master- og doktorgradsnivå.* Oslo, Abstrakt forlag, pp. 228–248.

Dysthe, O. and Samara, A. eds. (2006) *Forskningsveiledning på master- og doktorgradsnivå.* Oslo, Abstrakt forlag.

Dysthe, O., Hertzberg, F. and Hoel, T.L. (2000) *Skrive for å lære. Skriving i høyere utdanning.* Oslo, Abstrakt forlag.

Dysthe, O., Samara, A. and Westrheim, K. (2006) En treleddet veiledningsmodell i masterstudiet. In: Dysthe, O. and Samara, A. eds. *Forskningsveiledning på master- og doktorgradsnivå.* Oslo, Abstrakt forlag, pp. 37–55.

Engelsen, B.U. (2006) *Kan læring planlegges? Arbeid med læreplaner – Hva, hvordan, hvorfor?* Oslo, Gyldendal Norsk Forlag.

Fagerli, H.M. (2000) *En arena for læring og samhandling: Om bibliotekfaglige og pedagogiske utfordringer i læringssentermodellen.* HiO-rapport 4. Oslo, Høgskolen i Oslo.

Foster, A. (2004) A nonlinear model of information-seeking behavior. *Journal of the American Society for Information Science and Technology*, 55(3), 228–237.

Fourie, I. (1999) Empowering the users – current awareness on the Internet. *The Electronic Libray* (Internet), 17(6), 379–388. Available from: http://www.emeraldinsight.com/10.1108/02640479910329996 (Accessed 16 February 2008).

Habermas, J. (2006) *Preisrede von Jürgen Habermas anlässlich der Verleihung des Bruno-Kreisky-Preises für das politische Buch 2005* (Internet), 9 March. Renner Institut, University of Wien, Austria. Available from: www.renner-institut.at/download/texte/habermas2006–03–09.pdf (Accessed 12 February 2008).

Handal, G. and Lauvås, P. (1999) *På egne vilkår: en strategi for veiledning med lærere*. Oslo, Cappelen.

Handal, G. and Lauvås, P. (2006) *Forskningsveilederen*. Oslo, Cappelen.

Harvey, L. (2004–2007) *Analytic quality glossary* (Internet), Quality Research International. Available from: http://www.qualityresearchinternational.com/glossary/ (Accessed 16 February 2008).

High Level Colloquium on Information Literacy and Lifelong Learning (2005) *Beacons of the information society. The Alexandria proclamation on information literacy and lifelong learning* (Internet), Bibliotheca Alexandrina, Egypt, 6–9 November. Available from: http://www.bibalex.org/infolit2005/Proclamation/alexproceng.doc (Accessed 14 December 2005).

Hiim, H. and Hippe, E. (1993) *Læring gjennom opplevelse, forståelse og handling*. En studiebok i didaktikk. Oslo, Universitesforlaget.

Hughes, H., Bruce, C. and Edwards, S. (2007) Models for reflection and learning: a culturally inclusive response to the information literacy imbalance. In: Andretta, S. ed.

Change and challenge. Information literacy for the 21st century. Adelaide, Auslib Press, pp. 59–84.

Jackson, P.W. (1968) *Life in classrooms*. New York, Holt, Rinehart & Winston.

Kamler, B. & Thomson, P. (2006) *Helping doctoral students write. Pedagogies for supervision*. London, Routledge.

Karjalainen, A., Alha, K. and Jutila, S. (2006) *Give me time to think – determining student workload in higher education* (Internet), Teaching Development Unit, University of Oulu, Finland. Available from: http://www .oulu.fi/w5w/tyokalut/GET2.pdf (Accessed 3 December 2007).

Kuhlthau, C.C. (2004) *Seeking meaning. A process approach to library and information services*. 2nd edition. Westport, Libraries Unlimited.

Kvale, S. (1997) Research apprenticeship. *Nordisk pedagogik*, **17**(3), 186–194.

Lander, R.I. (2004) Management of educational innovation. In: Smelser, N.J. and Baltes, P.B. eds. *International encyclopedia of the social and behavioral sciences*. Amsterdam, Elsevier, pp. 4259–4261.

Lave, J. and Wenger, E. (1991) *Situated learning. Legitimate peripheral participation*. Cambridge, Cambridge University Press.

Lee, A. (1998) Doctoral research as writing. In: Higgs, J. ed. *Writing qualitative research*. Five Docks, Australia, Hampden Press. Quoted in: Dysthe, O., Samara, A. and Westrheim, K. (2006) En treleddet veiledningsmodell i masterstudiet. In: Dysthe, O. and Samara, A. eds. *Forskningsveiledning på master- og doktorgradsnivå*. Oslo, Abstrakt forlag, p. 49.

Lindén, J. (1998) *Handledning av doktorander*. Nora, Bokförlaget Nya Doxa. Quoted in: Handal, G. and Lauvås, P. (2006) *Forskningsveilederen*. Oslo, Cappelen, pp. 58–60.

Lorenzo, G. and Dziuban, C. (2006) Ensuring the Net Generation is Net Savvy. *ELI Paper* 2 (Internet), September. EDUCAUSE. Available from: http://www.educause.edu/ir/library/pdf/ELI3006.pdf (Accessed 1 February 2008).

Løvlie, L. (1972). Universitetspedagogikk – eller debaten som ble vekk. In: Mediaas, N. *et al.* eds. *Etablert pedagogikk – makt eller avmakt?* Oslo, Gyldendal, pp. 29–35.

Løvlie, L. (1974) Pedagogisk filosofi for praktiserende lærere. *Pedagogen,* 1 (22), 19–36.

Massialas, B.G. (2001) Hidden curriculum in the classroom. In: Smelser, N.J. and Baltes, P.B. eds. *International encyclopedia of the social & behavioral sciences.* Amsterdam, Elsevier, pp. 6683–6685.

McGuinness, C. (2007) Exploring strategies for integrated information literacy. From 'academic champions' to institution-wide change. *Communications in Information Literacy* (Internet), 1, 26–38. Available from: http://www.comminfolit.org/index.php/cil/article/view/Spring2007AR3/14 (Accessed 15 February 2008).

Miles, D.H. (2003) *The 30-second encyclopedia of learning and performance. A trainer's guide to theory, terminology and practice.* New York, AMACOM, American Management Association.

Piaget, J. (1971) *Biology and knowledge.* Chicago, University of Chicago Press.

Pressley, M., Borkowski, J.G. and Schneider, W. (1987) Cognitive strategies: Good strategy users coordinate metacognition and knowledge. In: Vasta, R. and Whitehurst, G. eds. *Annals of child development,* Vol. 4. Greenwich, CT, JAI Press, pp. 89–19.

Rafste, E.T. (2001) *Et sted å lære eller et sted å være? En case-studie av elevers bruk og opplevelse av skolebiblioteket.* Ph.D. thesis, University of Oslo. Oslo, Unipub.

Rafste, E.T. and Sætre, T.P. (2004) Bridging gaps – pedagogical investment. *Library Review*, 53(2), 112–118.

Skagen, T., Torras, M.C., Hafstad, S., Hunskår, I., Kavli, S. and Mikki, S. (2008) Pedagogical considerations in developing an online tutorial in information literacy. *Communications in Information Literacy* (in press) Available from: http://www.comminfolit.org/.

Stenhouse, L. (1975) *An introduction to curriculum research and development.* London, Heineman.

Sætre, T.P. (2002) *Biblioteket som læringsarena med bibliotekaren som pedagog: Et utviklingsarbeid knyttet til bibliotekarutdanning med sikte på å etablere et nytt fagområde kalt 'bibliotekpedagogikk'.* Høgskolen i Bergen Skriftserien 3. Bergen, Høgskolen i Bergen.

Sætre, T.P. (2007) Bibliotekets rolle i studentenes læringsarbeid. In: Wilhelmsen, B.U. and Hole, G.O. eds. *Læring for profesjonskompetanse.* Høgskolen i Bergen Skriftserien 2. Bergen, Høgskolen i Bergen, pp. 145–159.

The British Library and JSIC (2008) *Information behaviour of the researcher of the future.* CIBER briefing paper (Internet), The British Library and JSIC, UK. Available from: *http://www.bl.uk/news/pdf/googlegen.pdf* (Accessed 5 February 2008).

Throndsen, I.S. (2002) Selvregulert læring av matematikkferdigheter på begynnertrinnet. In: Bråten, I. ed. *Læring i sosialt, kognitivt og sosialt-kognitivt perspektiv.* Oslo, Cappelens Forlag, pp. 194–212.

Torras, M.C. and Skagen, T. (2006) User education at the digital library: physical and intellectual access to information through digital literacy. In: Garnes, K., Landøy, A. and Repanovici, A. eds. *Aspects of the digital library.* Laksevåg, Norway, Alvheim and Eide, pp. 75–86.

Torras, M.C. and Skagen, T. (2007) *Search and Write ('Søk & Skriv'): Helping postgraduate students with their academic work* (Internet), workshop presented at the Librarians' Information Literacy Annual Conference (LILAC), 26–28 March 2007, Manchester Metropolitan University, UK. Available from: http://www.cilip.org .uk/specialinterestgroups/bysubject/informationliteracy/lilac/ lilac2007/parallels.htm (Accessed 31 July 2007).

Van Deusen, J.D. (1996) The school library media specialist as a member of the teaching team: 'Insider' and 'outsider'. *Journal of Curriculum and Supervision*, **11**(3), 249–258.

Walker Rettberg, J. (2007) *Født som nettbruker. Bruk av blog og wiki blant dagens studenter* (Internet), paper presented at the seminar on Flexible Learning, 15–16 November, Oslo, Norway. Available from: http://www .slideshare.net/jilltxt/fdt-som-nettbruker-166320/ (Accessed 5 February 2008).

White, H.S. (1992) Bibliographic instruction, information literacy, and information empowerment. *Library Journal*, **January**, 76–78.

Wood, D., Bruner, J. and Ross, G. (1976) The role of tutoring in problem-solving. *Journal of Child Psychology and Psychiatry and Allied Disciplines*, **17**(2), 89–100.

Index